INVASION!

D-DAY & OPERATION OVERLORD
IN ONE HUNDRED MONENTS

SCOTT ADDINGTON

UNIFORM

Also available:
Reaching for the Sky
One Hundred Defining Moments from the
Royal Air Force 1918-2018
ISBN 978-1-911604-45-7

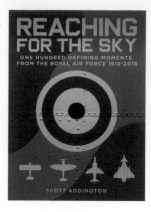

First published in 2019 by
Uniform, an imprint of Unicorn Publishing Group LLP
5 Newburgh Street
London
W1F 7RG
www.unicornpublishing.org

This edition first published by Uniform in 2019

Copyright © 2019 Scott Addington

Every effort has been made to trace copyright
holders and to obtain their permission for the use
of copyrighted material. The publisher apologises
for any errors or omissions and would be grateful
to be notified of any corrections that should be
incorporated in future reprints or editions of this book.

A catalogue record for this book is available from the
British Library

ISBN 978-1-912690-00-8

10 9 8 7 6 5 4 3 2 1

Designed by Matt Carr
Printed in Slovenia by Latitude Press

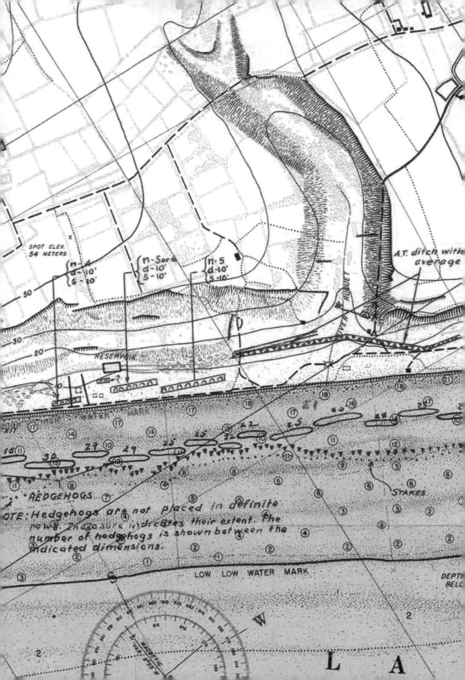

SPOT ELEV.
54 METERS

50

n-4
d-10'
S-30'

n-5or6
d-10'
S-10'

n-5
d-10'
S-10'

A.T. ditch with
average

30

20

RESERVOIR

WATER MARK

HEDGEHOGS

STAKES

OTE: Hedgehogs are not placed in definite
rows. Enclosure indicates their extent. The
number of hedgehogs is shown between the
indicated dimensions.

LOW LOW WATER MARK

DEPT
BELC

W

L A

INVASION!

D-DAY & OPERATION OVERLORD
IN ONE HUNDRED MONENTS

THE ACHIEVEMENT OF OPERATION
OVERLORD IS NEARLY IMPOSSIBLE TO
OVERSTATE, IN ITS CONSEQUENCES
FOR OUR OWN LIVES AND THE
LIFE OF THE WORLD.

THIS IS FOR ALL THOSE
WHO PARTICIPATED.

Contents

Introduction

I must have annoyed my publisher somehow...

This is the only reason I can think of as to why, after already giving me one seemingly impossible task (coming up with one hundred defining moments of the RAF for *Reaching for the Sky*) they follow that up by telling me to come up with a selection of one hundred key moments from what could be described as one of the most critical times of the entire 20th Century for western Europe. Namely, D-Day and the Battle for Normandy.

I mean, where do I start? 7,000 ships carrying more than 150,000 brave souls towards five landing beaches (plus Pointe du Hoc); a massive parachute drop behind enemy lines; sabotage by the bucket-load, brand new weapons; a programme of deception that was almost as big as the invasion itself; thousands of individual stories of tragedy, bravery and heroism and some of the most recognisable photographs of the modern era. And that was just day one!

So, after a great deal of head scratching and deliberation, here are my defining moments of D-Day and Operation Overlord. I have followed a similar pattern to *Reaching for the Sky* in as much as I have included a mix of moments that span very different aspects of the operation including planning and organisation, key personalities from both sides, technology and of course some jaw-dropping moments of courage.

The result is a very subjective and personal list, which you may not totally agree with. Despite that, I hope the stories told within this book inspire you the reader to search out more D-Day stories. I hope they encourage you to watch documentaries, visit museums, and even travel to Normandy and follow in the footsteps of the invasion. By doing this we will all help to keep the incredible stories and memories of this momentous piece of history alive.

Scott Addington

01 Timeline

5 June 1944
22:00
Operation Neptune commences. Five naval assault groups depart English ports.

6 June 1944
00:00
Operation Titanic (part of Operation Fortitude) begins, designed to confuse the German defenders about the exact place of the invasion. RAF aircraft drop hundreds of dummy paratroopers across the northern French coastline.

00:05
Allied air forces begin bombing coastal batteries between Le Havre and Cherbourg.

00:10
Reconnaissance groups and Pathfinders are dropped by parachute across the British and US airborne drop zones beyond the landing beaches.

00:20
British airborne forces under the command of Major Howard land in Horsa Gliders to begin attacks on various bridges over the River Orne and the Caen Canal.

00:35
Howard and his men successfully capture all bridges within fifteen minutes.

00:50
Paratroopers from the British 6th Airborne Division are dropped over Merville and Ranville to knock out the huge Merville Battery.

01:00
US 82nd Airborne Division commence parachute drop to the west of Sainte-Mére-Église.

01:11
First reports of American airborne assault reach HQ of German 84th Army Corps (based at St Lô).

01:30
US 101st Airborne Division commence parachute drop near Utah Beach.

01:50
Main body of British 6th Airborne Division commence parachute drop east of the River Orne.

02:45
Infantry troops heading for Omaha and Utah beaches begin to transfer from assault ships to landing craft.

03:00
Allied warships arrive at assigned positions ready for coastal bombardment. Allied air forces commence their attack on inland defences.

03:20
Heavy equipment and reinforcements for paratroopers arrive by glider.

03:25
German naval observers report presence of Allied task force forming off the coast of Normandy.

03:50
British paratroopers begin attack on the village of Ranville.

04:30
Paratroopers of 505th Regiment, US 82nd Airborne Division capture Sainte-Mére-Église.

04:40
Von Rundstedt orders the 12th SS Panzer Division to move immediately to Calvados.

04:45
Miniature submarines X-20 and X-23 surface to provide navigational reference points for landing craft destined for the British landing beaches. British paratroopers led by Colonel Terence Otway knock out the Merville Battery.

05:27
Allied warships begin shelling German coastal fortifications.

06:00
The BBC broadcasts a message to the people of Normandy from General Eisenhower, suggesting that they leave the area as quickly as possible.

06:30
Landings begin on Utah and Omaha beaches by the US VII Corps and V Corps. At the same time, General Jodl cancels the order from von Rundstedt ordering the 12th SS Panzer Division to mobilise – he decides it is better to wait for Hitler to wake up.

06:52
Admiral Ramsay, waiting anxiously at Southwick House, receives the first reports regarding conditions on the beaches.

07:00
German radio broadcasts initial report of the landings.

07:10
US Army 2nd Rangers Battalion begin assault at Pointe du Hoc.

07:25
British 3rd Infantry Division commences landings at Sword Beach. At the same time, the 50th Infantry Division hit Gold Beach.

07:35
Canadian 3rd Infantry Division commence landings on Juno Beach.

07.40
After hours without a decision, and with Hitler still sleeping, General Edgar Feuchtinger orders his 21st Panzer Division to move towards the eastern beaches.

08:00
Significant German resistance on Sword Beach finally supressed by British 3rd Division troops.

09:00
General Eisenhower authorises the release of the official announcement of the invasion to the general public.

09:13
The situation on Omaha Beach is desperate. General Bradley requests immediate reinforcements and seriously considers an evacuation or diverting troops to Utah Beach.

09:30
The BBC broadcasts Communique No.1 – the first official announcement of D-Day.

09:45
Utah Beach cleared of enemy forces.

10:00
British forces advancing inland from Gold Beach, occupy La Riviére.

10:45
The German 21st Panzer Division receives orders to attack Bayeux and Caen.

11:00
Canadian forces advancing inland from Juno Beach occupy the town of Berniéres.

12:00
British Prime Minister, Winston Churchill, reports on the invasion during a speech to the House of Commons. At the same time, units of the US 4th Infantry Division make contact inland with paratroopers from the US 101st Airborne Division near the town of Pouppeville.

13:00
British Commandos under Lord Lovat, advancing from Sword Beach, link up with Major Howard and his British airborne troops holding the bridges over the Orne.

13:30
US troops on Omaha Beach start to slowly move inland.

14:30
German 21st Panzer Division launches counterattack towards the invasion beaches.

15:00
German 12th SS Panzer Division takes up positions south of Caen.

16:00
British tanks reach Arromanches.

16:05
American armour begins advancing inland from Omaha Beach. The first US Sherman tank to reach the road connecting the beach to Colleville is quickly destroyed.

18:00
St Laurent, a town behind Omaha Beach, is liberated. At the same time, the Canadian 3rd Infantry Division from Gold Beach links up with the British 50th Division from Gold Beach. An address by Charles de Gaulle, recorded earlier that day, is broadcast across France.

20:00
German 21st Panzer Division reaches the coast at Luc-sur-Mer between Juno and Sword invasion beaches but is met by British armour and infantry.

21:00
British 6th Airborne Brigade lands by glider in drop zones around the River Orne.

22:00
Rommel returns to his Normandy HQ after being in Germany. Anglo/Canadian advance on Caen is held up in the Forest of Lebisay.

00:00 Midnight
D-Day ends. 159,000 Allied troops, marines, airmen and naval personnel have successfully established four sizeable beachheads. The invasion front remains vulnerable to German counterattack, but a crucial step has been taken towards the liberation of Europe.

02 Führer Directive No. 40

On 23 March 1942 Adolf Hitler issued his order, under Führer Directive No. 40, concerning the defence of the west.

All responsibility for the defence of the German-occupied territories in the west was handed over to Field Marshal Karl Rudolf Gerd von Rundstedt in his role as Commander in Chief West, reporting directly into OKW (Oberkommando der Wehrmacht). This was the beginning of a large split in the German High Command structure and by the beginning of 1943 the OKW became directly responsible for all western theatres while the OKH (Oberkommado der Heer) became responsible for the fighting in the east.

This co-ordination seemed practical on paper, however with key figures such as Admiral Raeder and Reichsmarschall Hermann Göring manoeuvring over and above this organisational structure due to their close relationship with Hitler, the ability of OKW or OKH to organise truly co-ordinated operations across the all three armed services, was practically impossible.

After the huge offensive in the east had ground to a halt, Hitler now faced his nightmare scenario — a war on two fronts. Furthermore, in the west he was facing a combined British, Canadian and American force that was building up significantly over in Britain.

Directive No. 40 was officially titled Command Organisation of the Coasts but was essentially the order to construct what would become known as the Atlantic Wall. He instructed his commanders, 'In the days to come the coasts of Europe will be seriously exposed to the danger of enemy landings…. Special attention must be paid to British preparations for landings on the open coast, for which numerous armoured landing craft suitable for the transportation of combat vehicles and heavy weapons are available. Large-scale parachute and glider operations are likewise to be expected.'

Constructing a casemate —
work begins on what became known as
the Atlantic Wall.

The Führer
and Supreme Commander
of the Armed Forces

TOP SECRET

26 Copies
Copy No. ...
OKW/WFSt/Op.Nr.: 001042 g.Kdos.

Directive No. 40

Subj: Command Organisation
of the Coasts

GENERAL SITUATION:

In the days to come the coasts of Europe will be seriously exposed to
the danger of enemy landings.

The enemy's choice of time and place for landing operations will
not be based solely on strategic considerations. Reverses in other
theatres of operations, obligations toward his allies, and political
motives may prompt the enemy to arrive at decisions that would be
unlikely to result from purely military deliberations.
Even enemy landing operations with limited objectives will - insofar
as the enemy does establish himself on the coast at all - seriously
affect our own plans in any case. They will disrupt our coastwise
shipping and tie down strong Army and Luftwaffe forces which
thereby would become unavailable for commitment at critical points.
Particularly grave dangers will arise if the enemy succeeds in taking
our airfields, or in establishing airbases in the territory that he
has captured.

Moreover, our military installations and war industries that are in
many instances located along or close to the coast, and which in part
have valuable equipment, invite local raids by the enemy.
Special attention must be paid to British preparations for landings
on the open coast, for which numerous armoured landing craft suitable
for the transportation of combat vehicles and heavy weapons are
available. Large-scale parachute and glider operations are likewise
to be expected.

GENERAL TACTICAL INSTRUCTIONS FOR COASTAL DEFENCE:

Coastal defence is a task for the Armed Forces, and requires
particularly close and complete co-operation of all the services.
Timely recognition of the preparations, assembly, and approach of the
enemy for a landing operation must be the goal of the intelligence
service as well as that of continual reconnaissance by Navy and
Luftwaffe.

Embarkation operations or transport fleets at sea must subsequently
be the target for the concentration of all suitable air and naval
forces, with the object of destroying the enemy as far off our coast
as possible.

However, because the enemy may employ skilful deception and take
advantage of poor visibility, thereby catching us completely by
surprise, all troops that might be exposed to such surprise operations
must always be fully prepared for defensive action.
Counteracting the well-known tendency of the troops to relax their
alertness as time goes on will be one of the most important command
functions.

Recent battle experiences have taught us that in fighting for the
beaches – which include coastal waters within the range of medium
coastal artillery – responsibility for the preparation and execution
of defensive operations must unequivocally and unreservedly be
concentrated in the hands of one man.

All available forces and equipment of the several services, the
organisations and formations outside of the armed forces, as well as
the German civil agencies in the zone of operations will be committed
by the responsible commander for the destruction of enemy transport
facilities and invasion forces. That commitment must lead to the
collapse of the enemy attack before, if possible, but at the latest
upon the actual landing.

An immediate counterattack must annihilate landed enemy forces, or
throw them back into the sea. All instruments of warfare – regardless
of the service, or the formation outside of the armed forces to
which they might belong – are to be jointly committed toward that
end. Nevertheless, shore-based Navy supply establishments must not
be hampered in their essential functions, nor Luftwaffe ground
organisations and Flak protection of airfields impaired in their
efficiency, unless they have become directly affected by ground combat
operations.

No headquarters and no unit may initiate a retrograde movement in such
a situation. Wherever Germans are committed on or near the coast, they
must be armed and trained for active combat.

The enemy must be kept from establishing himself on any island which in enemy hands would constitute a threat to the mainland or coastwise shipping.

Disposition of forces and improvement of fortifications are to be so made that the main defensive effort lies in those coastal sectors that are the most probable sites for enemy landings (fortified areas).

Those remaining coastal sectors that are vulnerable to coups de main of even small units must be protected by means of a strongpoint type of defence, utilising, if possible, the support of shore batteries. All installations of military and military-economic importance will be included in that strongpoint defence system.

The same rules apply to offshore islands. Coastal sectors that are less endangered will be patrolled.

The several services will establish a uniform definition of coastal sectors, if necessary, on the basis of a final decision on the part of the responsible commander named in III.) 1.) below.

By means of proportionate allocation of forces, improvement of positions (perimeter defence), and stockpiling of supplies, the fortified areas and strongpoints must be enabled to hold out even against superior enemy forces for extended periods of time. Fortified areas and strongpoints are to be held to the last. They must never be forced to surrender because of a shortage of ammunition, rations, or water.

The commander responsible according to III.) 1.) below, issues orders for coastal security, and assures a speedy evaluation, collation, and dissemination to authorised headquarters and civil agencies of intelligence procured by all the services.

Upon the first indication of an imminent enemy operation, that commander is authorised to issue the necessary orders for unified and complementary reconnaissance by sea and air.

All elements stationed in the vicinity of the coast, whether headquarters or units of the Armed Forces, or organisations or formations outside of the Armed Forces, will forego the niceties of peacetime protocol. Their quarters, security measures, equipment, state of alert, and utilisation of local resources will be governed solely by the necessity of countering every enemy raid with the utmost speed and force. Wherever the military situation demands, the civilian population will be evacuated at once.

COMMAND:

The following authorities are responsible for the preparation and
conduct of defence on coasts under German control: in the Eastern
Theatre of Operations (excluding Finland), the army commanders
designated by OKH; in the coastal sector under the control of Army
Lapland, the Commanding General of Army Lapland; in Norway, the Armed
Forces Commander, Norway; in Denmark, the Commander of German Troops
in Denmark; in the occupied West (including the Netherlands), the
Commander in Chief West; In matters pertaining to coastal defence,
the commanders mentioned in categories d) and e) above are under
the direct control of OKW; in the Balkans (including the occupied
islands), the Armed Forces Commander Southeast; in the Baltic and the
Ukraine, the Armed Forces Commanders Baltic and Ukraine;
in the Zone of Interior, the commanding admirals.

Within the framework of coastal defence missions, the commanders
designated in III.) 1.) above, will have command authority over
tactical headquarters of the services, the German civil authorities as
well as units and organisations outside of the armed forces that are
located within their respective areas. In exercising that authority,
the commanders will issue tactical, organisational, and supply orders
necessary for coastal defence, and insure their execution. They will
influence training to whatever extent is necessary for preparing their
forces for ground operations. The required data will be put at their
disposal.

Orders and measures implementing this directive will give priority to
the following: inclusion within fortified areas or strongpoints of all
installations important militarily or to the war economy, particularly
those of the Navy (submarine bases) and the Luftwaffe; unified
direction of coastal surveillance; infantry defences of fortified
areas and strongpoints; infantry defences of isolated installations
outside of fortified areas and strongpoints, such as coastal patrol
and aircraft warning stations; artillery defences against ground
targets (in installing new shore batteries and displacing those in
position, the requirements of naval warfare will receive priority);
defence preparedness of fortified establishments, their structural
improvement, and the stockpiling of reserve supplies, as well as
defensive preparedness and stockpiling of supplies in isolated
installations outside of those establishments (including supply
with all weapons necessary for defence, mines, hand grenades,
flame throwers, obstacle material, and similar items); signal
communications; tests of the state of alert as well as infantry and
artillery training within the framework of the defensive missions.
Similar authority will be vested in the commanders of local
headquarters down to sector commands, insofar as they have been made
responsible for the defence of coastal sectors.

The commanders enumerated in III.) 1.) above, will generally confer such responsibilities on commanding generals of army divisions that are committed for coastal defence, and in Crete, on the Fortress Commander Crete.

In individual sectors and subsectors, and particularly in establishments that have definitely been designated as air or naval bases, the local Luftwaffe or Navy commanders are to be put in charge of the entire defence, insofar as their other missions permit them to assume those responsibilities.

Naval and strategic air forces are subject to the control of the Navy or Luftwaffe, respectively. However, in case of enemy attacks on the coast they are - within the framework of their tactical capabilities - bound to comply with requests from the commanders responsible for defensive operations. For that reason, they must be included in the exchange of military intelligence, in preparation for their future employment. Close contact must be maintained with their respective higher headquarters.

Special missions of the several services within the framework of coastal defence:

NAVY:

organisation and protection of coastwise shipping; training and commitment of the entire coastal artillery against sea targets; commitment of naval forces.

LUFTWAFFE:

air defence in the coastal areas. This mission does not affect the right of local defence commanders to direct the assembly of Flak artillery suited and available for commitment against enemy invasion forces. improvement of the Luftwaffe ground organisation and its protection against air and surprise ground attacks on airfields that have not been sufficiently protected by their inclusion in the coastal defence system. commitment of strategic air forces.
Instances of overlapping control resulting from those special missions must be accepted as unavoidable.
As of 1 April 1942, all instructions and orders not in agreement with the present directive are rescinded.
New combat directives issued by the responsible commander pursuant to my directive will be submitted to me through OKW.

signed:

Adolf Hitler

03 The Atlantic Wall

In the same speech in the Reichstag on 11 December 1941, where he declared war on the USA, Hitler also mentioned for the first time his vision for making Europe an 'impregnable fortress'. He went on to boast with much gusto that

...from Kirkenes (on the Norwegian/ Finnish border) to the Spanish frontier stretches the most extensive belt of great defence installations and fortresses.... I am determined to make this European front impregnable against any enemy attack.

It was a bold claim; the length of territory mentioned in this speech was almost 3,000 miles, but Hitler was insistent and on 23 March 1942 he issued 'Führer Directive No. 40' which, in anticipation of a large-scale Allied invasion, stipulated that the Atlantic coastal defences should be designed in such a way that any invasion attempt would be smashed to pieces either before the main landing force had a chance to reach land or immediately afterwards. He wanted 15,000 concrete strong-points manned by 300,000 soldiers, and as no one really knew where the invasion would occur, the whole of the coastline had to be defended.

Field Marshal Karl Gerd von Rundstedt was given the challenge of putting all of this together and was given fourteen months in which to complete it.

Thousands upon thousands of slave labourers, staff from the German state construction organisation (Organisation Todt), and civilian workers sourced from local populations were forced to work twenty-four hours a day, building the concrete fortifications, gun emplacements, pill-boxes and assorted other structures that made up the Wall. The requirement for basic construction materials was so great that parts of the French Maginot Line and the German Siegfried Line were dismantled and used to bolster the Atlantic Wall. Despite this, the deadline of 1 May 1943 came and went – it had always been an unrealistic target.

By the autumn of 1943 around half a million men were working on the construction of the Atlantic Wall, but it was not enough, and progress was still very slow. Field Marshal von Rundstedt asked Hitler for more resources to help finish the job. In response to this request Hitler sent Rommel. Rommel was also given an explicit directive to evaluate and inspect the coastal defences of the rest of the Atlantic Wall and report back directly to the Führer's headquarters with his findings.

His report back was less than complimentary. The Wall was nowhere near ready and would not stand a chance against any kind of invasion. Rommel was of the opinion that the invasion battle would be won and lost on the beaches, so with the backing of both

Hitler and von Rundstedt, he got busy building a defensive structure that might have a chance to stop any invasion force in its tracks.

On every beach that could feasibly handle an invasion force, huge numbers of anti-invasion obstacles were erected, such as jagged sections of steel girders, concrete bollards and metal-tipped wooden stakes, many of which were adorned with anti-tank Teller mines or artillery shells that were primed to explode with just the slightest impact. These were placed just below high- and low-tide water marks and were specifically designed to rip apart troop-filled landing craft.

In and around the beaches – especially on inland pathways – Rommel had his men sow immense minefields designed to stop any invasion force penetrating too far too fast. By the summer of 1944, approximately five million mines of various designs had been planted and it was behind these mine-belts that Rommel's men took up their positions in concrete bunkers, gun emplacements and pill-boxes. They were all linked together using underground tunnels and included offices, latrines, kitchens, water and ventilation systems and first aid posts. Thick belts of barbed wire and yet more minefields encircled these strongpoints in such a way as to funnel any attacking force into killing zones covered by machine-gun nests with interlocking fields of fire.

Further inland, great tracts of land were purposefully flooded to hinder enemy paratroopers. Any area within seven or eight miles of the coast that could be used as landing grounds for gliders were covered with large heavy wooden stakes nicknamed Rommelspargeln (Rommel's asparagus). These stakes were booby-trapped with explosives and trip wires.

Field Marshal Rommel had organised the most hostile welcoming party ever seen. There was nothing left for him to do but wait for the inevitable. He knew the Allies were coming. He just did not quite know where or when.

The Atlantic Wall

- **Fortifications**
- **Occupied**
- **Allied**
- **Neutral**

Rommel tours Atlantic Wall defences in France.

Field Marshal General Erwin Rommel inspects the strengthening
of the Atlantic Wall near the French city of Sangatte.

1.2

million tons of steel went into the Atlantic Wall. That is enough to build more than

20,000

Tiger tanks

= 1,000 tanks

The 'wall' was really a three-tier system of fortifications running almost 3,000 miles from the Franco-Spanish border all the way to the northern tip of Norway. Strategic port cities, like Cherbourg, Brest and Antwerp, were to become festungen or 'fortresses'

Only

10%

of the men forced to build the Atlantic Wall were German

By the summer of 1944, the Nazis had laid more than

5

million mines along the Atlantic Wall.

=$1 billion

The cost to lay down just the French portion of the Atlantic Wall was 3.7 billion Reichsmarks

That's

$206

billion in today's currency

04 Führer Directive No. 51

Field Marshal von Rundstedt issued a report on the state of the Western defences on 25 October 1943 – it did not paint a pretty picture. There were twenty-seven infantry divisions stationed along the Atlantic coast at this time, but most of these divisions only consisted of two inexperienced and largely immobile infantry regiments. In addition to this, there was a severe shortage of artillery support and the majority of the panzer divisions in the area were still in the process of being re-fitted after service in the east. Rundstedt also made it clear that the Kriegsmarine and Luftwaffe were strong enough in the west to counter growing Allied air and sea superiority.

On 3 November 1943, a week after von Rundstedt's report was submitted, Hitler issued Directive No. 51, which resulted in a flurry of activity among German planners during the last two months of 1943, as they started to make plans to make western coastal forces more mobile and to increase the speed in which local panzer units were upgraded. Hitler's Directive was partially a reaction to von Rundstedt's report, but partially due to a growing conviction along the German corridors of power that, following the military reverses suffered by the Wehrmacht in the east and south, the Allies must surely be girding their loins for some action in the west. Therefore, there could be no more compromises in the west in order to favour other theatres of war, the Atlantic coastal defences would now be given priority. It would now be forbidden to transfer armoured units out of the west without Hitler's express approval and both the Luftwaffe and Kriegsmarine were ordered to up their game in the west to give the coastal defence units the back-up they needed.

This Directive heralded a new dawn of focus and attention to the defensive preparations in the west, as Hitler awaited the 'decisive struggle in the west'.

Grenadiers from the German 130 Panzer Lehr Division in a Sd.Kfz.251 armoured personnel carrier, near Caen, France.

Albumwar2.com

The Führer
and Supreme Commander
of the Armed Forces

27 Copies
Copy No. ...
OKW/WFSt/Op.N. 662656/43 g.K.Chefs
Directive No. 51
Subj: Defence of the West

Führer Headquarters
3 November 1943

DIRECTIVE NO.51

For the last two and one-half years the bitter and costly struggle
against Bolshevism has made the utmost demands upon the bulk of our
military resources and energies. This commitment was in keeping
with the seriousness of the danger, and the over-all situation. The
situation has since changed. The threat from the East remains, but an
even greater danger looms in the West: the Anglo-American landing! In
the East, the vastness of the space will, as a last resort, permit a
loss of territory even on a major scale, without suffering a mortal
blow to Germany's chance for survival.

Not so in the West! If the enemy here succeeds in penetrating our
defences on a wide front, consequences of staggering proportions will
follow within a short time. All signs point to an offensive against
the Western Front of Europe no later than spring, and perhaps earlier.
For that reason, I can no longer justify the further weakening of the
West in favour of other theatres of war. I have therefore decided to
strengthen the defences in the West, particularly at places from which
we shall launch our long-range war against England. For those are the
very points at which the enemy must and will attack; there – unless
all indications are misleading – will be fought the decisive invasion
battle.

Holding attacks and diversions on other fronts are to be expected. Not
even the possibility of a large-scale offensive against Denmark may
be excluded. It would pose greater nautical problems and could be less
effectively supported from the air, but would nevertheless produce the
greatest political and strategic impact if it were to succeed.

During the opening phase of the battle, the entire striking power of the enemy will of necessity be directed against our forces manning the coast. Only an all-out effort in the construction of fortifications, an unsurpassed effort that will enlist all available manpower and physical resources of Germany and the occupied areas, will be able to strengthen our defences along the coasts within the short time that still appears to be left to us. Stationary weapons (heavy AT guns, immobile tanks to be dug-in, coast artillery, shore-defence guns, mines, etc.) arriving in Denmark and the occupied West within the near future will be heavily concentrated in points of main defensive effort at the most vulnerable coastal sectors. At the same time, we must take the calculated risk that for the present we may be unable to improve our defences in less threatened sectors.

Should the enemy nevertheless force a landing by concentrating his armed might, he must be hit by the full fury of our counter-attack. For this mission ample and speedy reinforcements of men and materiel, as well as intensive training must transform available larger units into first-rate, fully mobile general reserves suitable for offensive operations. The counter-attack of these units will prevent the enlargement of the beachhead, and throw the enemy back into the sea. In addition, well-planned emergency measures, prepared down to the last detail, must enable us instantly to throw against the invader every fit man and machine from coastal sectors not under attack and from the home front. The anticipated strong attacks by air and sea must be relentlessly countered by Air Force and Navy with all their available resources. I therefore order the following:

ARMY:

The Chief of the Army General Staff and the Inspector General of Panzer Troops will submit to me as soon as possible a schedule covering arms, tanks, assault guns, motor vehicles, and ammunition to be allocated to the Western Front and Denmark within the next three months. That schedule will conform to the new situation. The following considerations will be basic:

Sufficient mobility for all panzer and panzer grenadier divisions in the West, and equipment of each of those units by December 1943 with 93 Mark IV tanks or assault guns, as well as large numbers of antitank weapons.

Accelerated reorganisation of the 20 Air Force Field Divisions into an effective mobile reserve force by the end of 1943. This reorganisation is to include the issue of assault guns.

Accelerated issue of all authorised weapons to the SS Panzer Grenadier
Division Hitler Jugend, the 21st Panzer Division, and the infantry and
reserve divisions stationed in Jutland.

Additional shipments of Mark IV tanks, assault guns, and heavy AT guns
to the reserve panzer divisions stationed in the West and in Denmark,
as well as to the Assault Gun Training Battalion in Denmark.

In November and December, monthly allotments of 100 heavy AT guns
models 40 and 43 (half of these to be mobile) in addition to those
required for newly activated units in the West and in Denmark.

Allotment of large numbers of weapons (including about 1,000 machine-
guns) for augmenting the armament of those static divisions that are
committed for coastal defence in the West and in Denmark, and for
standardising the equipment of elements that are to be withdrawn from
sectors not under attack.

Ample supply of close-combat AT weapons to units in vulnerable
sectors.

Improvement of artillery and AT defences in units stationed in
Denmark, as well as those committed for coastal protection in the
occupied West. Strengthening of GHQ artillery.

The units and elements stationed in the West or in Denmark, as well
as panzer, assault gun, and AT units to be activated in the West,
must not be transferred to other fronts without my permission. The
Chief of the Army General Staff, or the Inspector General of Panzer
Troops will submit to me a report through the Armed Forces Operations
Staff as soon as the issue of equipment to the panzer and assault gun
battalions, as well as to the AT battalions and companies, has been
completed.

Beyond similar measures taken in the past, the Commander in Chief West
will establish timetables for, and conduct manoeuvres and command
post exercises on, the procedure for bringing up units from sectors
not under attack. These units will be made capable of performing
offensive missions, however limited. In that connection I demand that
sectors not threatened by the enemy be ruthlessly stripped of all
forces except small guard detachments. For sectors from which reserves
are withdrawn, security and guard detachments must be set aside from
security and alarm units. Labour forces drawn largely from the native
population must likewise be organised in those sectors, in order to
keep open whatever roads might be destroyed by the enemy air force.

The Commander of German Troops in Denmark will take measures in the
area under his control in compliance with paragraph 3 above.

Pursuant to separate orders, the Chief of Army Equipment and Commander of the Replacement Army will form Kampfgruppen in regimental strength, security battalions, and engineer construction battalions from training cadres, trainees, schools, and instruction and convalescent units in the Zone of the Interior. These troops must be ready for shipment on 48 hours' notice.

Furthermore, other available personnel are to be organised into battalions of replacements and equipped with the available weapons, so that the anticipated heavy losses can quickly be replaced.

AIR FORCE:

The offensive and defensive effectiveness of Air Force units in the West and in Denmark will be increased to meet the changed situation. To that end, preparations will be made for the release of units suited for commitment in the anti-invasion effort, that is, all flying units and mobile Flak artillery that can be spared from the air defences of the home front, and from schools and training units in the Zone of the Interior. All those units are to be earmarked for the West and possibly Denmark.

The Air Force ground organisation in southern Norway, Denmark, north-western Germany, and the West will be expanded and supplied in a way that will – by the most far-reaching decentralisation of own forces – deny targets to the enemy bombers, and split the enemy's offensive effort in case of large-scale operations.

Particularly important in that connection will be our fighter forces. Possibilities for their commitment must be increased by the establishment of numerous advance landing fields. Special emphasis is to be placed on good camouflage. I expect also that the Air Force will unstintingly furnish all available forces, by stripping them from less threatened areas.

NAVY:

The Navy will prepare the strongest possible forces suitable for attacking the enemy landing fleets. Coastal defence installations in the process of construction will be completed with the utmost speed. The emplacing of additional coastal batteries and the possibility of laying further flanking mine fields should be investigated.

All school, training, and other shore-based personnel fit for ground combat must be prepared for commitment so that, without undue delay, they can at least be employed as security forces within the zone of the enemy landing operations.

While preparing the reinforcement of the defences in the West, the Navy must keep in mind that it might be called upon to repulse simultaneous enemy landings in Norway and Denmark. In that connection, I attach particular importance to the assembly of numerous U-boats in the northern area. A temporary weakening of U-boat forces in the Atlantic must be risked.

SS:

The Reichsfuehrer-SS will determine what Waffen-SS and police forces he can release for combat, security, and guard duty. He is to prepare to organise effective combat and security forces from training, replacement, and convalescent units, as well as schools and other home-front establishments.

The commanders in chief of the services, the Reichsfuehrer-SS, the Chief of the Army General Staff, the Commander in Chief West, the Chief of Army Equipment and Commander of the Replacement Army, the Inspector General of Panzer Troops, as well as the Commander of German Troops in Denmark will report to me by 15 November all measures taken or planned.

I expect that all agencies will make a supreme effort toward utilising every moment of the remaining time in preparing for the decisive battle in the West.

All authorities will guard against wasting time and energy in useless jurisdictional squabbles, and will direct all their efforts toward strengthening our defensive and offensive power.

signed:

Adolf Hitler

05 Casablanca

When the Casablanca Conference opened on 12 January 1943, the Allied leaders felt for the first time that they were able to dictate when and where to next take the war to the enemy. Rommel had been all but defeated in the African desert, the Russians were on the offensive in the east and in the Pacific, Japanese expansion had finally been stemmed.

There was, however, still one big cause for concern – the German U-Boat presence in the Atlantic. In 1942 1,027 Allied ships were sunk by enemy submarines and without control of the seas the US would not be able to influence the war in the west. Even worse, without substantial US manufactured equipment the Allies could not even begin to dream of undertaking a large enough amphibious landing needed to open operations in the west.

Churchill was still of the opinion that in the light of such problems the Allies should concentrate their efforts on operations in the Mediterranean, where a smaller invasion could take place quicker and had more chance of being successful. This would especially be so if Italy could be knocked out of the war and he could persuade Turkey to let the Allies use their country as a base from which to launch an attack on the vital Romanian oil fields.

The US General Marshall did not agree and saw the Mediterranean plan as nothing more than a small tactical diversion. He was of the opinion that the defeat of Germany would only come about with direct military action against the main body of the German Army in the west, and the priority should be to plan for this – anything else was merely a diversion from the true strategic imperative of ultimate victory in Europe.

The debate was lively and intense, with both sides not willing to give in. However, eventually the US Chiefs of Staff agreed that current circumstances meant that an operation in the Mediterranean was better than no operation at all, and agreed, in principal, to an attack on Sicily. Even though he had yielded, General Marshall still made it clear that he wished northern France to be the battleground of the main attack against the enemy.

The question of defeating Germany was not the only item on the agenda at Casablanca. It was clear that Japan was still a formidable foe and it was agreed that there should be a substantial increase in offensive activity in the Pacific throughout 1943. This meant that American resources would be prioritised for the Pacific; for the attack on Sicily, Churchill would have to make do with the resources he would be given.

The main attention of Casablanca was on military operations of 1943. Indeed, it was declared that the military operations planned for 1943 would bring about the defeat of Germany in the same year.

However, not many of the Allied leaders truly believed that 1943 would see the end of the war and the Combined Chiefs of Staff set up a planning committee to look at the possibility of small-scale continental raids in 1943 and a larger invasion in 1944.

Over the next six months the groundwork for a full-scale invasion of France was completed – transforming it from a collection of ideas to a proper plan of action, scoped out with the necessary men and materials.

Did you know

The Casablanca Conference was the first time an American president had left American soil during wartime

US National Archives

Casablanca Conference, 14—24 January 1943. President Franklin D. Roosevelt, Prime Minister Winston S. Churchill and their Combined Chiefs of Staff at the Casablanca Conference.

06 Early Plans: Roundup & Sledgehammer

On 22 June 1941, the Wehrmacht smashed its way through the Russian frontier across a 500-mile front. The advance was staggering even by Blitzkrieg standards and Soviet losses were equally impressive. As Churchill publicly welcomed Russia into the arms of the Allies, joined together in their fight against a common enemy, the reply from Moscow was characteristically terse. After more than three weeks' radio silence, Stalin sent his first message to Churchill on 18 July 1941, demanding that a second front be opened to help relieve the pressure on his own army.

The subject of a second front had been a topic of hot conversation among Allied commanders since Dunkirk. In October 1941, Churchill told Captain Lord Louis Mountbatten to prepare for the invasion of Europe, explaining that, 'Unless we can go on land and fight Hitler and beat his forces, we shall never win this war.' On the other side of the Channel, the German top brass also knew that the fighting would eventually heat up in the west, hence the frantic building of the Atlantic Wall.

The question was not if there would be an invasion but when and where.

The US was keen to get to France as quickly as possible and had drawn up comprehensive invasion plans by as early as mid-1942. Forty-eight infantry divisions would attack, of which eighteen would be British, backed up by almost 6,000 aircraft. These men would be dropped off by 7,000 landing craft somewhere between Boulogne and Le Havre. This would be backed up by a smaller invasion force consisting of ten British Divisions who would aim to occupy the Cherbourg Peninsula. Everything would be ready by April 1943 – speed was everything, just in case the Russians collapsed under the weight of the Nazi advance in the east.

Churchill accepted the plans in principle. The invasions were even given code names: 'Roundup' was to be the name for the larger invasion, with 'Sledgehammer' the name given to the smaller British-led attack on Cherbourg.

The problem was that, despite Churchill's agreement, British commanders hated the idea and regarded these plans as suicidal. Many of them had had first-hand experience of large assaults against formidable enemies during World War 1 and were keen to avoid any deadly repeats.

When Soviet Foreign Minister, Vyacheslav Molotov passed on a message from Stalin on 20 May 1942 demanding the urgent opening of a second front to divert at least forty Wehrmacht divisions from the east, the pressure was really starting to mount for Churchill and

President Roosevelt. The Americans wanted to press full steam ahead with both Roundup and Sledgehammer but Churchill had had a change of heart and instead pushed for an invasion of North Africa as being a more viable second front option.

The Allies eventually agreed that they did not have enough landing craft at the time, and in August 1942 abandoned the concept in favour of 'Torch' using the same scale of forces but in a theatre of less possible resistance and thus able to exert a direct influence on the outcome of the war, in this instance North Africa where large numbers of French troops were also based and might therefore assist the Allied cause.

> 'No responsible British General, Admiral or Air Marshal is prepared to recommend Sledgehammer as a practical operation in 1942'

Winston Churchill, in a wire to President Roosevelt, 8 June 1942

Did you know

The plans for Operation Roundup was drawn up by then Brigadier General Dwight D. Eisenhower

Bigger than Overlord

The original plan for Operation Roundup called for a force of 48 Allied Divisions, backed up by 5,800 aircraft. Operation Overlord featured just 39 Divisions

Divisions

Aircraft

5,800

11,000

48 **39**

● Roundup ● Overlord

US Library of Congress

A jeep rolls off a landing boat at Fedala Harbour in Morocco during the landing operations of the US forces during Operation Torch.

07 COSSAC

At the Casablanca Conference in January 1943 it was agreed between the Allied leaders that the work of preparing for the grand assault on Fortress Europe should start in earnest and be shared between Britain and the USA. In order to kick-off the planning, Lieutenant General Sir Frederick Morgan was appointed to the post of Chief of Staff to the Supreme Allied Commander (COSSAC) with Brigadier General R.W. Baker of the US Army named as his deputy.

In late April 1943, Morgan and his COSSAC staff were given a three-pronged brief.

First, Morgan was to prepare a plan for a diversionary attack against the Pas de Calais to dupe the Germans into thinking this would be the main attack and so encouraging them to concentrate their defences in the wrong position. Secondly, he was to plan Operation Rankin, a quick and sudden cross-Channel attack of a smaller scale to help out Russia if needed or to exploit any perceptible weakness in the enemy. Thirdly, the priority role for COSSAC would be to begin preparations for '... a full-scale assault against the Continent in 1944 as early as possible'. This was Operation Overlord.

The first big question facing COSSAC was where to attack. The Nazis held almost 3,000 miles of Western European coastline, but after a full examination of aerial reconnaissance photographs, tidal charts and on-the-ground reports,

Morgan and his staff narrowed it down to just two areas of French coast: the Pas de Calais and Normandy. The former was closer to England but was much more heavily defended. Normandy, on the other hand, was sheltered from the unpredictable Channel weather by the Cherbourg peninsula, boasted wide beaches with suitable exits for vehicles, and there was open land lying beyond that could provide airfields. Taking all of this into consideration, Normandy was tentatively selected as the invasion destination of choice.

In May 1943, senior COSSAC figures sold the plan to Prime Minister Churchill and during the same month Morgan was told that the Combined Chiefs of Staff had selected a date of 1 May 1944 as the date of the invasion, giving the COSSAC team just one year to plan the most ambitious and outrageous military operation in history.

During the next twelve months Morgan worked miracles to get the prerequisite materials and resources in place, often sleeping on a camp bed at night in his office. Incredibly, he submitted the first draft of his invasion plan to the British chiefs of staff in mid-July 1943 - that first draft would go on to provide a solid foundation for ultimate success.

Organisational Chart

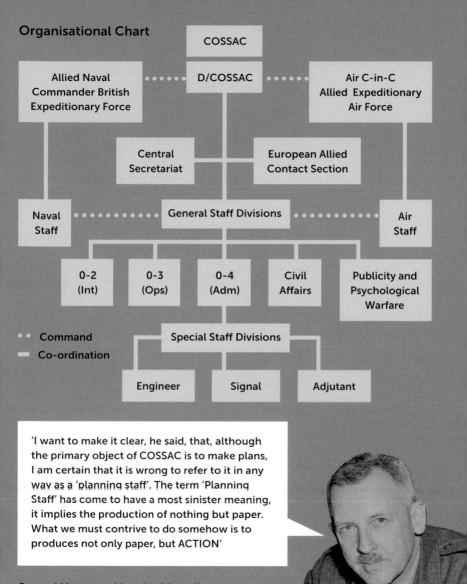

```
                          COSSAC
                             │
  Allied Naval          D/COSSAC          Air C-in-C
  Commander British    · · · · · · ·      Allied Expeditionary
  Expeditionary Force                     Air Force
                             │
              Central              European Allied
              Secretariat         Contact Section
                             │
  Naval      · · · · · · ·  General Staff Divisions  · · · · · · ·   Air
  Staff                                                              Staff
              │            │            │            │            │
           0-2          0-3          0-4          Civil        Publicity and
           (Int)        (Ops)        (Adm)        Affairs      Psychological
                                                               Warfare
                             │
                       Special Staff Divisions
              │                    │                    │
           Engineer             Signal               Adjutant
```

· · Command
▬   Co-ordination

'I want to make it clear, he said, that, although the primary object of COSSAC is to make plans, I am certain that it is wrong to refer to it in any way as a 'planning staff'. The term 'Planning Staff' has come to have a most sinister meaning, it implies the production of nothing but paper. What we must contrive to do somehow is to produces not only paper, but ACTION'

General Morgan, addressing his staff during the first meeting of COSSAC held on 17 April 1943

35

08 COPP: Beach Reconnaissance & Confirmation

On paper, the Normandy coast seemed to tick all the invasion boxes – apart from one. There were rumours that underneath the sand was a layer of peat, if true this could cause huge issues for some of the larger vehicles coming ashore, which could sink through the sand and get stuck in the peat. The big question that needed answering was this: could the beaches in this region cope with tanks, trucks, bulldozers and other heavy vehicles that would be needed during the landings?

There was only one way to find out – someone had to go to those beaches and collect samples.

That job fell to the men of No. 1 Combined Operations Pilotage and Beach Reconnaissance Party (COPP), namely Major Logan Scott-Bowden and Sergeant Bruce Ogden-Smith who swam ashore to take samples of the sands on a beach that would later be given the code name 'Gold'. It was New Year's Eve 1943. Disembarking from their midget submarine a quarter of a mile from land, Scott-Bowden and Ogden-Smith swam ashore carrying various small arms and a dozen twelve-inch test tubes. This mission was so dangerous they were both offered cyanide capsules – both had refused, even though they knew if they were discovered they would face certain death.

Keeping within the high tide mark so the sea would wash away their prints, they crawled along the sand taking samples, noting the location of each sample on waterproof writing tablets. As they worked, they could hear the local German garrison singing as they celebrated the New Year. On leaving, they had to negotiate waves sweeping them back to shore. This was not an easy night's work, but they managed it without major incident.

Back in England, the beach samples were closely examined. The results were good - the Normandy sand would be able to cope with the heavy traffic of an invasion force.

Similar missions were carried out on the other beaches – Sword, Juno, Utah, and the trickiest of all, Omaha, which presented a high bluff to be scaled beyond the sand. Scott-Bowden and Ogden-Smith reconnoitred Omaha in January 1944, based for four days in a midget X20 submarine, emerging at night to take samples.

When Scott-Bowden was summoned to speak to a dozen admirals and generals at Norfolk House in London's St James's Square, he had a simple message for Bradley: 'Sir, I hope you don't mind me saying it, but this beach [Omaha] is a very formidable proposition indeed and there are bound to be tremendous casualties.' Bradley replied, 'I know, my boy, I know.'

Standard COPP equipment

Bags for shingle samples and an auger tube for taking core samples from beaches

A fishing line on reel attached to a 1 ft brass rod for distance from shore measurements

A waterproof small compass

Various pockets and pouches containing equipment such as emergency rations and flares

Rope-soled fishermen's boots

Weapons include fighting knife and a revolver in holster, which had to be stripped and cleaned after each sortie

Wet suit with watertight fit around exposed face, reinforced elbows and knees (for crawling), buoyancy control.

Matt white slate for underwater writing

Diver's watch

Waterproof torch with blue lens

'As we swam back through heavy surf towards our rendezvous point, I thought [Ogden-Smith] was in trouble, when I heard him shouting. But when I turned to help, he only wished me "Happy New Year". I told him to "swim you b*****, or we'll land back on the beach"'

Major Scott-Bowden

In June 1944 the total number of personnel (all ranks) in COPP was

174

09 Choosing a Leader

The choice of an overall leader for the Allied forces was always going to be tough decision to make. National politics and strong personalities were going to make such an appointment very difficult, and so it turned out to be.

Churchill had resigned himself to the fact that any leader would be an American. The fact that the US Army would represent approximately half of the total invasion force made this a simple inevitability, but who would be chosen to lead the men on to the beaches? President Roosevelt was leaning towards giving the top seat to General Marshall. Marshall had transformed the US Army from a small group of men totalling just 170,000 in 1939 into the finest and best-equipped fighting machine on the planet in just three years. However, he was also Roosevelt's chief military advisor and had developed an outstanding reputation within Congress – he had become somewhat indispensable in Washington. This, and due to the fact, he had not gone public and asked to be considered for the position, meant he was passed over. Instead, he was selected as *Time* magazine's 'Man of the Year' and given a fifth star along with the title 'General of the Army'.

The only other US General who was considered to possess the required qualities to lead an entire expeditionary force was General Dwight D. Eisenhower. Eisenhower was at least a known quantity and had a good track record in leading invasions – he had commanded three of them already in the war, all of them involved British and American land, sea and air forces. He was also well respected by the British high command. He was, on paper at least, the perfect man for the job. On 7 December 1943, Eisenhower met President Roosevelt in Tunis. It was here that the President turned to Eisenhower and told him the news. 'Well, Ike, you are going to command Overlord.' Eisenhower replied, 'Mr President, I hope you will not be disappointed.'

The decision was made almost by default. General Dwight D. Eisenhower would be the Supreme Commander Allied Expeditionary Force.

'General of the Army'
Dwight D. Eisenhower
16 January 1944 – 26 November 1945.

10 Directive for Operation Overlord

Eisenhower took up his new command on 15 January 1944. His original headquarters were in London, but he disliked being there as Churchill and other dignitaries who were also based in the capital thought nothing of calling in to see 'how he was doing' at any time of the day or night. It was too distracting, so by the end of the month he had moved his HQ to Bushy Park, far enough outside the city to avoid these interruptions.

On 12 February 1944 he received an official Directive, outlining his role as Supreme Commander Allied Expeditionary Force in eight succinct paragraphs:

Eisenhower meets with his commanders in London, January 1944.

Left to right: Lieutenant General Omar Bradley, commanding US Army Ground Force: Admiral Sir Bertram Ramsay, Allied Naval Commander; Air Chief Marshal Sir Arthur Tedder, Deputy Supreme Commander; General Dwight D. Eisenhower, Supreme Commander; General Bernard Montgomery, Commander in Chief; Air Chief Marshal Sir T. Leigh-Mallory; Lieutenant General Walter Bedell Smith, US Army.

DIRECTIVE

CLASSIFIED

To Supreme Commander Allied
Expeditionary Force

(Issued 12 February 1944)

1. You are hereby designated as Supreme Allied Commander of the forces placed under your orders for operations for liberation of Europe from Germans. Your title will be Supreme Commander Allied Expeditionary Force.

2. Task. You will enter the continent of Europe and, in conjunction with the other United Nations, undertake operations aimed at the heart of Germany and the destruction of her armed forces. The date for entering the Continent is the month of May 1944. After adequate channel ports have been secured, exploitation will be directed towards securing an area that will facilitate both ground and air operations against the enemy.

3. Notwithstanding the target date above you will be prepared at any time to take immediate advantage of favorable circumstances, such as withdrawal by the enemy on your front, to affect a re-entry into the Continent with such forces as you have available at the time; a general plan for this operation when approved will be furnished for your assistance.

4. Command. You are responsible to the Combined Chiefs of Staff and will exercise command generally in accordance with the diagram at Appendix (reproduced on following page). Direct communication with the United States and British Chiefs of Staff is authorized in the interest of facilitating your operations and for arranging necessary logistical support.

5. Logistics. In the United Kingdom the responsibility for logistics organization, concentration, movement and supply of forces to meet the requirements of your plan will rest with British Service Ministries so far as British Forces are concerned. So far as United States Forces are concerned, this responsibility will rest with the United States War and Navy Departments. You will also be responsible for coordinating the requirements of British and United States Forces under your command.

6. Coordination of operations of other Forces and Agencies. In preparation for your assault on enemy occupied Europe, Sea and Air Forces agencies of sabotage, subversion and propaganda, acting under a variety of authorities are now in action. You may recommend any variation in these activities which may seem to you desirable.

7. Relationship with United Nations Forces in other areas. Responsibility will rest with the Combined Chiefs of Staff for supplying information relating to operations of the Forces of the U.S.S.R. for your guidance in timing your operations. It is understood that the Soviet Forces will launch an offensive at about the same time as OVERLORD with the object of preventing the German forces from transferring from the Eastern to the Western Front. The Allied Commander in Chief, Mediterranean Theater, will conduct operations designed to assist your operation, including the launching of an attack against the south of France at about the same time as OVERLORD. The scope and timing of his operations will be decided by the Combined Chiefs of Staff. You will establish contact with him and submit to the Combined Chiefs of Staff you views and recommendations regarding operations from the Mediterranean in support of your attack from the United Kingdom. The Combined Chiefs of Staff will place under your command the forces operating in Southern France as soon as you are in a position to assume such command. You will submit timely recommendations compatible with this regard.

8. Relationship with Allied Governments. – the re-establishment of Civil Governments and Liberated Allied Territories and the administration of enemy territories. Further instructions will be issued to you on these subjects at a later date.

11 SHAEF

Almost immediately after being appointed Supreme Commander, Eisenhower returned to the US for a short break and several weeks of never-ending briefings and high-level strategy meetings. Simultaneously, there began an energetic search for the most gifted commanders and leaders that could support Eisenhower. British Air Chief Marshal Sir Arthur Tedder (Commander in Chief of Allied Air Forces in the Mediterranean) was nominated to be Eisenhower's deputy. Admiral Ramsay, who had masterminded the Dunkirk evacuation as well as the recent North African invasion, was appointed as Naval Commander and Air Marshal Sir Trafford Leigh-Mallory was given responsibility for the Allied Tactical Air Force.

Perhaps the most important appointment would be that of Ground Force Commander of the Allied Armies, who would be responsible for getting the men off the beaches safely in the face of a full-on German counterattack. Eisenhower desperately wanted to appoint Field Marshal Harold Alexander, the British General who had done much to solidify Anglo-American operations in North Africa, but Churchill did not want to move him away from his current position on the Italian Front. Second choice was General Sir Bernard Montgomery, with American Generals Omar Bradley and Jacob Devers commanding the US 1st Army and the US 12th Army Group respectively.

Eisenhower returned to London in mid-January and on 15 January 1944 sat down at his desk for the first time as Supreme Commander Allied Expeditionary Force. Within a month, his Supreme Headquarters Allied Expeditionary Forces (known also as SHAEF), replaced and absorbed the COSSAC planning group.

Originally, SHAEF was located in the centre of London but Eisenhower quickly relocated his HQ to a quieter area on the outskirts of the capital, in Bushy Park. Very quickly a canvas town was created as SHAEF rapidly grew into a large and complex machine – by 1944 it boasted some 750 officers and over 6,000 staff members all working towards one unified goal: achieving a successful seaborne landing on the Calvados coast and the subsequent liberation of France and the rest of Western Europe.

A plaque now commemorates the location of SHAEF HQ in Bushy Park.

SHAEF shoulder patch

Upon a field of heraldic sable (BLACK), representing the darkness of Nazi oppression, is shown the sword of liberation in the form of a crusader's sword, the flames arising from the hilt and leaping up the blade. This represents avenging justice by which the enemy power will be broken in Nazi-dominated Europe. Above the sword is a rainbow, emblematic of hope, containing all the colours of which the national flags of the Allies are composed

The heraldic chief of azure (BLUE) above the rainbow is emblematic of a state of peace and tranquillity, the restoration of which to the enslaved people is the objective of the United Nations

'There was of course great secrecy about what was happening within the park. In the press everyone sensed that the much talked about Second Front was soon to commence. But when it did so on that Tuesday morning of 6th June 1944, it came as a surprise. There was much activity within the camp and all-day communiqués were read out over the tannoy system surrounding the camp, which enabled us to hear how Operation Overlord was progressing. We sat on our bunks thinking over the volumes of typing we had each done and now it was happening, especially when we heard place names being given in the news bulletins'

Edna Stafford (nee Hodgson) Administrator / Typist: SHAEF.

12 BIGOT

When Eisenhower arrived in London after his appointment as Supreme Commander, he urged everyone, including the British Government, to take extensive security measures in an effort to keep details of the invasion as secret as possible. Eisenhower warned his men:

The rules of security are known to us all – a guarded tongue and safeguarded documents. It rests with each of us to ensure that there is no relaxation of these rules until success is achieved. All commanders will ensure that the highest standard of individual security discipline is maintained throughout their commands, and that the most stringent disciplinary action is taken in all cases of the violations of security.

A special level of protection was put in place for all documents that mentioned the time and place of the invasion. A new secrecy classification was introduced that

Those on the BIGOT list were banned from travelling outside the UK in case they were captured and coerced into talking. There was just one exception to this – Prime Minister Churchill

was even more secret than 'Top Secret' – called 'BIGOT'. Only the privileged few were cleared to view documents labelled 'BIGOT' and they were labelled as being 'Bigoted'. To gain entry into this very select club was tough – the most thorough security checks were made on likely candidates on both sides of the Atlantic and after clearance anyone who was Bigoted was always open to having their behaviour closely scrutinised.

The odd codename was derived from the stamp 'To Gib' that had appeared on the papers of all officers travelling to Gibraltar for Operation Torch, the invasion of North Africa in 1942. The letters were simply reversed in order to confuse anyone snooping around.

Graphic Conservation Co.

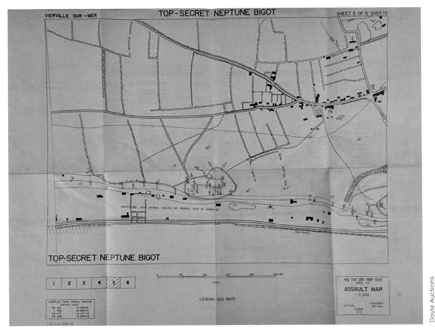

13 Choosing a date for D-Day

Choosing the exact date and timing of the invasion was most definitely a collective decision with the Combined Chiefs of Staff co-ordinating closely with their Russian friends. Considerations were also given to the weather, tidal phases and the availability of equipment and resources.

In the revised Overlord plan, which was worked on extensively during the spring of 1944, the date of 1 June 1944 was highlighted as the target date. In reality, this meant that the actual invasion would take place as soon as possible after this date – the actual day would be determined by when favourable weather, tidal and light conditions would occur. However, trying to figure these aspects out with any degree of certainty was not easy.

One of the major questions was whether to attack at night or during the day. There were many potential advantages for a night assault. Darkness would conceal the size and strength of the invading forces and interfere with any enemy retaliation; however, the desire to engage in overwhelming naval and air bombardments in support of the attack meant that the invasion had to take place during daylight, as the effectiveness of such fire depended on accurate observation of selected targets. A such, it was decided that 'H-Hour' should be within one hour of first light, although this was subject to adjustments based on suitable tidal conditions.

Those tidal conditions were a constant source of significant head scratching for the folks involved in planning the attack. The tidal range across the invasion zone was about 7 m (23 ft). The landings had to take place on a rising tide to allow landing craft to ground, unload and withdraw without becoming stranded, but low tide on Omaha Beach uncovered a tidal flat of around 300 yards that would need to be crossed by the assaulting troops while being completely exposed to enemy small arms and artillery fire. Then there were the rocky outcrops lying off the beaches within the proposed British landing zones, which meant a landing at low tide would be impossible, but the landings across all of the beaches had to be roughly simultaneous to avoid alerting the enemy before the full force of the invasion could be applied. Eventually, it was decided that the time for the assault should be one hour after low tide.

To impose rigid light and tide conditions on to the invasion force would have been folly and would have placed the entire operation at the mercy of the weather, so there was a certain amount of flexibility baked in to the plans. For example, the daylight window for H-Hour was set at between 30 and 90 minutes after first light.

The required combination of favourable light and tide conditions occurred for only six days per month. A further requirement of strong moonlight to aid the planned airborne operations narrowed the window to just three days per month. As such, the first possible D-Days following the operational target date were 5, 6 and 7 June.

Arthur Thomas Doodson, Oceanographer

Arthur Thomas Doodson, head of the Liverpool Tidal Institute, had been giving the Royal Navy tidal information for various European coastal areas for months before he received a letter from Royal Naval Commander Ian Farquharson in October 1943 asking him to measure tidal conditions in a new position, cryptically named 'Position Z'. Doodson created two tide-prediction machines which made accurate tidal predictions for 'Position Z' — which turned out to be the Normandy coast — possible and thus successfully highlighted the small window of opportunity for the invasion of between 5–7 June 1944

Royal Society

Arthur Thomas Doodson, 1890–1968.

14 Briefing at St Paul's School

On 15 May, a full three weeks before the great invasion was due to take place, the great and the good of the Allied war machine met together in the bowels of St Paul's School, in west London. Eisenhower had gathered together the men who had planned D-Day and who would be responsible for its execution on 6 June. In attendance were numerous British chiefs of staff, the War Cabinet, scores of Allied generals and General Bernard Montgomery. During that meeting they would discuss and explain the plans for the invasion and, ultimately, the liberation of Europe, to none other than the British Prime Minister and King George VI.

The king sat in the front row, with Churchill on one side and Eisenhower on the other. To the left of Eisenhower were seated his deputies: Air Chief Marshal Tedder, Admiral Ramsay, General Montgomery, Air Chief Marshal Leigh-Mallory and Admiral Creasey. The rest of the room was filled to the brim with commanders, generals, air marshals, staff officers, and War Cabinet members. As everyone shuffled about to take their seats, the room hushed. It was cold in the room, war austerity meant there was no heating and many of the dignitaries shared blankets to keep themselves warm. As they waited for the conference to start, the tension became palpable. Everyone in the room was acutely aware of the importance of the gathering and what was at stake.

HAMMERSMITH AND FULHAM HISTORIC BUILDINGS GROUP

D-DAY 6 JUNE 1944
The Normandy landings were planned by General Montgomery and others in St Paul's School, which occupied this site from 1884 to 1968. On 15 May 1944 the final invasion plan was presented to General Eisenhower and senior allied commanders in the school lecture theatre, in the presence of King George VI and the Prime Minister, Winston Churchill.

2009

Alamy

Did you know

The map that Montgomery used during the briefing is still on display in the modern-day site of the school in the Montgomery Room

The boundary wall, gate pillars and the Highmaster's House are all that remain of the original St Paul's School buildings. There is, however, a Blue Plaque on the outer wall that commemorates the famous D-Day briefing

First on stage was the Supreme Commander. He spoke for around ten minutes with understated confidence and purpose. By the time he had finished, the tension in the room had disappeared. Next on stage was Montgomery, who took the audience through the basic objectives of the ground forces for D-Day, as well as the plan to move inland. During the rest of the conference each commander talked through his own particular role and task in the invasion. Once they had finished the Prime Minister gave one of his typical tub-thumping speeches. During the course of his speech he used an expression that struck a chord with many in attendance. He said, 'Gentlemen, I am hardening toward this enterprise.' During the conference Churchill had asked many questions and had dived deep into the detail of the operation – something he was prone to do under stress. Over the previous few years Churchill had been in support of an attack through the south of Europe, rather than into France directly. He still lived with the tragedy of Gallipoli from 1915 but it seemed that he had finally come around to believe that an invasion of France was the right course of action to take.

Lastly, the king himself rose and took his place on the platform. He was not expected to speak, he was not a natural public orator, a state of mind aggravated by a pronounced stammer, but he did so confidently and without notes. He was positive, upbeat and his speech made an excellent impression on his distinguished audience.

'During the whole war I attended no other conference so packed with rank as this one'

General Dwight D. Eisenhower

15 Invasion Stripes

During the planning phases of the invasion it was quickly discovered that the Identification, Friend or Foe system for identifying aircraft would not be able to cope with the thousands of machines that would be in the air at the time of the assault. During Operation Torch in 1942, Allied aircraft used yellow surrounds on their national insignia and it worked well – the concept of visual identification was thus already proven in combat.

On 17 May 1944, Air Chief Marshal Sir Trafford Leigh-Mallory approved the idea of using a similar painted aircraft identification system for Operation Overlord. A small test was carried out on 1 June, when planes bearing markings were flown over the Allied invasion fleet that was gathering in earnest off the southern coast of England. This helped familiarise ships' crews to the new markings, but the decision to paint the air

fleet was not officially issued until 4 June. Once the order was issued, nearly every Allied tactical aircraft in Great Britain was painted with 'invasion stripes' to prevent or reduce the prospect of friendly aircraft being shot down by Allied ground and sea forces. The invasion was originally scheduled for the 5 June, but it was delayed by 24 hours due to the weather. This delay allowed ground crews to paint more aircraft with the D-Day markings, which were three white stripes and two black, each between 8 and 18 in wide on the wings and fuselages, depending on the size of aircraft.

A month after the Normandy Landings, the stripes were removed from the tops of airplanes. Now that the invasion was over, the stripes would make the easy targets for the enemy. By the end of 1944 all markings, wherever they were on the planes, had been removed.

A Spitfire Mk.IX in D-Day invasion stripes.

Formation of Martin B-26Bs. Closest aircraft is B-26B-15-MA (S/N 41-31612). Note the invasion stripes.

Spitfire showing invasion stripes.

P-47 fighter-bomber pilots at a rough airstrip near Sainte-Mère-Église on 15 June 1944. By the end of August, all eighteen of the 9th Air Force's fighter-bomber and four of its medium bomber groups were based on the continent.

05:00

The first reports of the landings reach Hitler's summer retreat at the Berghof, Berchtesgaden, Bavaria. He has taken a sleeping pill so no one wakes him.

08:30

Albert Speer, Hitler's Armaments Minister is at the Berghof and is informed of the invasion. He asks if the Führer has been informed. An adjutant replies that he only receives news after he has eaten breakfast.

09:00

Hitler wakes and is told of the invasion. He is triumphant, being of the opinion that now the Allies are attempting to land in Europe his Wehrmacht can properly beat them at last. He is still convinced the landings are a diversionary tactic and calls for a military conference.

12:00

Hitler chairs an upbeat conference at the tea house in Kehlstein, about an hour's drive from the Berghof. Hitler tells his commanders that the weather is on Germany's side and he expects the Allied invasion to be pushed back into the sea quite easily. He orders the enemy to be 'annihilated' by the end of the day – to quash any risk of further landings. To many members of the German High Command present at that conference, Hitler seemed almost relieved that the invasion was finally happening.

16:00

Hitler finally gives his consent to release extra panzers to assist the 21st Panzer Division. He also gives the order to commence V1 rocket attacks on England at the earliest opportunity.

16:55 Hitler sends an order to Field Marshal von Rundstedt, stating that the 'enemy beachhead must be cleaned up no later than tonight'.

23:00 Hitler hosts a second conference with his military commanders. He tells his High Command that he is still convinced that the landings in Normandy are nothing more than a diversionary attack.
The Sicherheitsdienst, Hitler's security service, issues a memo on the mood of the German public, stating that the 'onset of invasion is widely experienced as a deliverance from unbearable tension and oppressive uncertainty. It constitutes the only topic of conversation.'

Did you know

The Germans had received so many false alarm reports of invasions throughout the summer of 1944 that when news reached the Berghof in the early hours of D-Day regarding the Allied landings no one was willing to wake Hitler in case it was yet another false report

17 We shall fight on the beaches

By 25 May 1940 the situation for the Allies was looking particularly bleak. Despite the best combined efforts of the French Army and the British Expeditionary Force (B.E.F.) they were unable to halt the German bulldozer and almost 400,000 Allied soldiers found themselves trapped and encircled on the beaches around the French coastal town of Dunkirk. The decision to evacuate as many men as possible away from the beaches was made quickly and over nine days between 27 May and 4 June, 332,226 men were successfully rescued. However, British losses were significant: 68,111 casualties (killed/wounded/captured) along with the loss of 243 ships, over 63,000 vehicles and over half a million tonnes of general supplies, ammunition and rations.

It all added up to a testing few days for the British Prime Minister, Winston Churchill who addressed the House of Commons on 4 June as the last of the men trapped at Dunkirk were brought back to England. He spoke for an hour, concluding his address with one of the most famous passages of oration in recent British history.

This defiance in the face of huge pressure set the tone for the next four years. The Allies may have been down, but they certainly were not out. They would be back and they would come back fighting ... 'on the beaches'. It may have been the summer of 1940, but already the seeds for D-Day had been sown.

Mixed reactions to the speech

In the House of Commons, some members were reduced to tears, but many members of the public were less convinced. According to the Ministry of Information's report on domestic morale at the time, there was only limited evidence that the speech had energised the public and in fact it generated a rather downbeat reaction:

'The grave tone of Churchill's speech made some impression and may have contributed in some measure to the rather pessimistic atmosphere of today.... The contents of the speech were on the whole expected, but some apprehension has been caused throughout the country on account of the PM's reference to "fighting alone". This has led to some slight increase in doubt about the intentions of our ally [France]'

... I have, myself, full confidence that if all do their duty, if nothing is neglected, and if the best arrangements are made, as they are being made, we shall prove ourselves once again able to defend our Island home, to ride out the storm of war, and to outlive the menace of tyranny, if necessary for years, if necessary alone. At any rate, that is what we are going to try to do. That is the resolve of His Majesty's Government – every man of them. That is the will of Parliament and the nation. The British Empire and the French Republic, linked together in their cause and in their need, will defend to the death their native soil, aiding each other like good comrades to the utmost of their strength.

Even though large tracts of Europe and many old and famous States have fallen or may fall into the grip of the Gestapo and all the odious apparatus of Nazi rule, we shall not flag or fail. We shall go on to the end, we shall fight in France, we shall fight on the seas and oceans, we shall fight with growing confidence and growing strength in the air, we shall defend our Island, whatever the cost may be, we shall fight on the beaches, we shall fight on the landing grounds, we shall fight in the fields and in the streets, we shall fight in the hills; we shall never surrender, and even if, which I do not for a moment believe, this Island or a large part of it were subjugated and starving, then our Empire beyond the seas, armed and guarded by the British Fleet, would carry on the struggle, until, in God's good time, the New World, with all its power and might, steps forth to the rescue and the liberation of the old.

Did you know?

The famous audio recording of this speech is actually from 1949, when Churchill was asked to record it for posterity. At the time of the original speech there was no way of broadcasting from the House of Commons

18 Hitler declares war on America

On 11 December 1941, just four days after the Japanese attack on Pearl Harbor, Adolf Hitler addressed the Reichstag in Berlin with an 88-minute speech which he had written himself. The speech, broadcast to the German nation, recounted the reasons for the outbreak of war in September 1939, explained why he decided to strike against the Soviet Union in June 1941, reviewed the dramatic course of the war thus far, and dealt at length with President Franklin Roosevelt's hostile policies toward Germany. Hitler detailed the increasingly belligerent actions of Roosevelt's government, and then dramatically announced that Germany was now joining Japan in the war against the United States:

Adolf Hitler addresses the Reichstag, 11 December 1941.

WikiCommons

... *Since the beginning of the war [in September 1939], the American President Roosevelt has steadily committed ever more serious crimes against international law. Along with illegal attacks against ships and other property of German and Italian citizens, there have been threats and even arbitrary deprivations of personal freedom by internment and such. The increasingly hostile attacks by the American President Roosevelt have reached the point that he has ordered the US navy, in complete violation of international law, to immediately and everywhere attack, fire upon and sink German and Italian ships. American officials have even boasted about destroying German submarines in this criminal manner. American cruisers have attacked and captured German and Italian merchant ships, and their peaceful crews were taken away to imprisonment in addition, President Roosevelt's plan to attack Germany and Italy with military forces in Europe by 1943 at the latest was made public in the United States [by the Chicago Tribune and several other newspapers on 4 December 1941] and the American government made no effort to deny it.*

Despite the years of intolerable provocations by President Roosevelt, Germany and Italy sincerely and very patiently tried to prevent the expansion of this war and to maintain relations with the United States. But as a result of his campaign, these efforts have failed.

Faithful to the provisions of the Tripartite Pact of 27 September 1940, Germany and Italy accordingly now regard themselves as finally forced to join together on the side of Japan in the struggle for the defence and preservation of the freedom and independence of our nations and realms against the United States of America and Britain.

This was the only time Hitler went to war with a country via a speech. Every other country was subjected to some kind of Blitzkreig attack – and perhaps, in retrospect, it was a declaration too far. In any case this declaration set in motion a series of complex events that would eventually cumulate in the greatest amphibious landings of all time.

19 Field Marshal Erwin Rommel

Erwin Rommel was a very different commander from von Rundstedt. His leadership of German and Italian forces in the North African Campaign established his reputation as one of the most able tank commanders of the war, and earned him the nickname der Wüstenfuchs (the Desert Fox). He was never accused of war crimes and he made sure Allied prisoners were treated fairly. As a result, he was respected by his enemies as well as his own men.

Born on 15 November 1891 in southern Germany, the young Rommel initially wanted to pursue a career in engineering, but his father disapproved and instead he joined the Imperial German Army. During the First World War he saw active service in France, Romania and Italy, was wounded three times, awarded Imperial Germany's highest decoration (the 'Pour le Merit') and established a reputation for himself as being a fearless and innovative commander in the field. Rommel further enhanced his reputation in France in 1940 where he was awarded the Knight's Cross of the Iron Cross in recognition of his expertise in the art of Blitzkrieg while commanding the 7th Panzer Division, but it was in North Africa commanding the Deutsches Afrika Korps where, despite defeat, he cemented himself as one of the most talented and celebrated leaders in the German Army.

After his exploits in the desert, Rommel was moved across to France to oversee the construction of the Atlantic Wall. When he saw the reality of the situation, with so much of the 'wall' incomplete, he devoted himself full time to bolstering the sea defences. He had millions of mines laid and thousands of tank traps and obstacles set up on the beaches and throughout the countryside. Yet despite all of this effort, the Atlantic Wall was never fully completed.

The bad weather at the beginning of June 1944 convinced Rommel that he could safely travel to Germany and spend a few days with his family and as the invasion forces gathered off the Normandy coast, he was at home celebrating his wife's birthday. Although he returned to France immediately on hearing the news of the invasion, there was very little he could do. After having a request to withdraw and reorganise refused, Rommel met with Hitler on 29 June, warning him that Germany was on the verge of defeat. Meanwhile a group of conspirators were developing a plot to assassinate Hitler and overthrow the government. They quietly approached Rommel and invited him to join their group; however, the Generalfeldmarschall refused the offer, explaining that he preferred to arrest Hitler and place him on public trial.

On 17 July, whilst returning from visiting the headquarters of the I SS Panzer Corps, Rommel's car was strafed by an RAF Spitfire, veering off the road and hitting a tree. Whilst Rommel was in hospital, recovering from his injuries, Claus von Stauffenberg carried out a failed assassination attempt on Hitler.

As the conspirators were rounded up and executed, Rommel's name kept coming up in the investigations. Hitler knew that having Rommel convicted and executed would be bad for morale, so instead, on 14 October he sent two senior staff officials, Wilhelm Burgdorf and Ernst Maisel, to Rommel's home to inform him of the situation and give him two options: he could either face the People's Court – which would have been tantamount to a death sentence – or choose a quiet suicide. If he chose the People's Court option, it was likely that his family and his staff would be arrested and executed as well. If he chose suicide, he was given assurances that his family would be protected, they would receive full pension payments, the government would claim he died a hero's death as a result of his injuries and he would be buried with full military honours.

Burgdorf had brought a cyanide capsule. Wearing his Afrika Korps jacket and carrying his field marshal's baton, Rommel quietly explained his decision to his wife and son and was driven away in a staff car where he was left alone in a remote location outside the village. Within five minutes he was dead. The German public were told he had died from wounds suffered in his recent car accident.

Awards

Military Merit Order (Württemberg)

Iron Cross 2nd Class

Iron Cross 1st Class

Pour le Mérite

Clasp to the Iron Cross 2nd Class

Clasp to the Iron Cross 1st Class

Knight's Cross of the Iron Cross

Oak Leaves

Swords (6th recipient)

Diamonds (6th recipient)

Italian Gold Medal of Military Valour

Knight of the Colonial Order of the Star of Italy

'Sweat saves blood, blood saves lives, but brains saves both'

20 Field Marshal Karl von Rundstedt

A Prussian officer who served during World War 1, Field Marshal Karl Rudolf Gerd von Rundstedt came out of retirement in 1939 to be one of Hitler's most senior commander of the Germany Army. In May 1939, he was appointed Commander of Army Group South and tasked with overseeing the invasion of Poland from Silesia and Slovakia. After the swift capitulation of Poland, he was put in charge of Army Group A during the invasion of France in 1940. His decision to delay the advance of the panzer divisions on Dunkirk in order to consolidate his positions enabled the evacuation of the trapped British Expeditionary Force across the English Channel. After France had requested an armistice with Germany, Hitler promoted von Rundstedt and a number of other field commanders to field marshal (Generalfeldmarschall) during the 1940 Field Marshal Ceremony. Von Rundstedt reiterated his wish for retirement but was persuaded by Hitler to stay on in France and oversee the planning for he proposed invasion of Britain, Operation Sealion.

In March 1942 von Rundstedt was given command of German forces in the west with responsibility for the defence of the northern European coast and the French Mediterranean coast against possible Allied attack. He had no confidence in the Atlantic Wall, preferring a 'defence in depth' strategy to repel any Allied invasion, but Hitler sent Rommel with the order to strengthen the Atlantic Wall so that any Allied landings would be thrown back into the sea.

When the invasion came, it was much further west than either von Rundstedt or Rommel had expected and there was very little in the way of German armour in the vicinity of the landings. Von Rundstedt ordered the 12th SS Panzer Division 'Hitler Jugend' and the Panzer Lehr Division to move up to the Normandy coast in response to the invasion and then sent a message to OKW (Oberkommando der Wehrmacht) telling them of the situation. He was told to halt the advance and await Hitler's decision, which did not come until the afternoon. By then it was too late.

Von Rundstedt was taken prisoner on 1 May 1945 and after the war was charged with war crimes but was not tried in person due to his age and failing health. He did, however, appear as a defence witness for the army high command. He died of heart failure on 24 February 1953, aged seventy-seven.

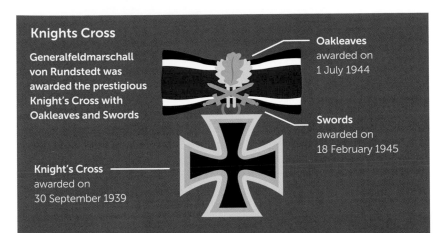

Knights Cross

Generalfeldmarschall von Rundstedt was awarded the prestigious Knight's Cross with Oakleaves and Swords

Oakleaves awarded on 1 July 1944

Swords awarded on 18 February 1945

Knight's Cross awarded on 30 September 1939

Macht Schluss mit dem Krieg, ihr Idioten! (Stop the war, you idiots!) After Hitler had reversed his orders, allowing a retreat of armoured forces around Caen that were being annihilated by Allied Naval gunfire, he phoned Wilhelm Keitel, urging him to speak to Hitler and get him to change his mind. Keitel said this was impossible and asked von Rundstedt what else could be done, to which he allegedly shouted 'Macht Schluss mit dem Krieg, ihr idioten!' (Stop the war, you idiots!)

German Commander in Chief West Karl Rudolf Gerd von Rundstedt (left) and Field Marshal Erwin Rommel at the George V hotel in Paris, France, 1943.

German Federal Archives

21 General George S. Patton

Strong-willed, combative and known for carrying pistols with ivory handles, General George Smith Patton, Jr is regarded as one of the most successful United States field commanders of any war.

Born on 11 November 1885 into a military family, he attended the Virginia Military Institute and graduated from the United States Military Academy at West Point on 11 June 1909. He was then commissioned a Second Lieutenant in the 15th Cavalry Regiment. He studied fencing, designing the M1913 Cavalry Sabre and was good enough to represent his country at the modern pentathlon in the 1912 Olympic Games in Sweden.

In April 1941 he was made Commanding General of the 2nd Armoured Division and in January 1942 he was given the command of I Armoured Corps and quickly established the Desert Training Centre in southern California. It would be the perfect place for his men to practise desert warfare, something that would come in very handy, as by November 1942 Patton was given the command of the 33,000 men that made up the Western Task Force, the only all-American force landing as part of Operation Torch, the Allied invasion of North Africa.

On 6 March 1943 Patton replaced Major General Lloyd Fredendall as the Commanding General of II Corps and was promoted to Lieutenant General. II Corps had just been handed a beating by

the Afrika Korps at the battle of Kasserine Pass, but Patton had orders to take the battered and bruised formation into action again in just ten days' time. Patton gave all his men a new, clean uniform to wear and immediately put them through their paces. He had an uncompromising leadership style and pushed his men hard, but he was effective. On 17 March the 1st US Infantry Division won the Battle of El Guettar to register America's first major victory against Nazi forces.

He then passed on his Command of II Corps to General Bradley before returning to Casablanca to help with the planning of Operation Huskey – the Allied invasion of Sicily – where he commanded the US Seventh Army in landing at Gela, Scoglitti and Licata in an effort to support the British Eighth Army. Despite being ordered to concentrate on protecting the left flank of the British forces, Patton took Palermo and Messina, but this success was overshadowed by reports of him slapping two soldiers who were suffering from PTSD, calling them cowards and ordering them back to the front line. Patton received fierce criticism back home in America and was forced to make a public apology.

After these incidents Patton spent a significant period of time without a command before being moved to England and assigned the task of getting the newly formed US Third Army ready for forthcoming invasion of Europe.

He was also given the role of Commander of the non-existent First US Army Group (FUSAG), which was part of the Allied deception plan to protect the details of the Normandy landings.

Patton's Third Army did not take part in D-Day, but sailed to Normandy throughout June and July 1944, before being officially operational on 1 August, forming the extreme western flank of the Allied invasion forces.

After the war in Europe had ended, Patton asked for a command in the Pacific but his request was denied. Instead, he was appointed as military governor of Bavaria and then given the command of the US Fifteenth Army based in Bad Nauheim. On 8 December 1945 he was involved in a car accident where he broke his neck. He died on 21 December.

> ## 'It's better to fight for something in life than to die for nothing'

George S. Patton

Lieutenant General George Patton (left) is discussing further actions with Lieutenant Colonel Lyle Bernard from the 30th Infantry Regiment near Brolo in Italy, 1943.

Third Army stats

Between becoming operational in Normandy on 1 August 1944 and the end of hostilities on 9 May 1945, the Third Army was in continuous combat for...

281
days

In that time, it crossed

24
major rivers

and captured

81,000

square miles (211,000 km²) of territory, including more than

12,000

cities and towns

22 General Henry Crerar

Henry Duncan Graham Crerar was born in Hamilton, Ontario, on 28 April 1888. He was educated at the Royal Military College in Kingston, Ontario, from 1906 to 1909 and then joined the Militia. During World War 1 he served with distinction with the Canadian Field Artillery, rising to the rank of Lieutenant Colonel and being awarded the Distinguished Service Order. Unlike many Canadian officers of the time, Crerar opted to remain in the service In Britain after war had finished, attending the Staff College, Camberley and then accepting a post on the General Staff of the War Office in London. In March 1939, with the possibility of another war looming, he was recalled to Canada to prepare a mobilisation plan.

At the outbreak of World War 2, Crerar was sent back to the Canadian Military Headquarters in London and made responsible for ensuring that the required equipment, barracks and training plans were in place when Canadian troops arrived. In July 1940, he was called back to Ottawa and was quickly promoted to Chief of General Staff. He took immediate measures to improve the efficiency of National Defence HQ and set up emergency recruitment and training programmes. The idea of conscription was not popular in Canada, especially with those of French descent who did not want to become involved in what was perceived as a British war. However, attitudes did change after the fall of France.

A farewell sign, posted on behalf of General H.D.G. Crerar to troops of the First Canadian Army departing the Netherlands in 1945, read:

Here's wishing you a satisfactory and speedy journey home, and that you find happiness at the end of it. You go back with your share of the magnificent reputation earned by the Canadians in every operation in which they have participated in this war. A fine reputation is a possession beyond price. Maintain it – for the sake of all of us, past and present – in the days ahead. I know that you will get a great welcome on your return. See to it that those Canadian units and drafts which follow after you get just as good a 'welcome home' when they also get back. Good luck to each one of you – and thanks for everything. (H.D.G. Crerar) General

Crerar was appointed to command the 2nd Canadian Division in 1942, and in 1943 briefly commanded the 1st Canadian Corps in Italy – his first taste of the battlefield since World War 1 – but after just a few months he was recalled back to England to take over command of the First Canadian Army and prepare them for the invasion of France. For the Normandy landings, the First Canadian Army was part of Montgomery's Twenty-First Army Group, later the British Second Army. Montgomery was unimpressed by the Canadian, and when Crerar was unable to attend an important briefing, he threatened to sack him.

The Canadians played a major part in the push inland from the Normandy beachheads, especially in the breakout through German defensive lines south and in Caen, and the encirclement of the German Army Group B at Falaise in August 1944. In November 1944, he was promoted to full general, leaving his mark on the largest army Canada ever levied.

Crerar retired from the military in 1946 but continued to work for his country, holding diplomatic roles in Czechoslovakia, the Netherlands and Japan. He died in Ottawa on 1 April 1965.

General H.D.G. Crerar

23 Lt. General Frederick Morgan

In the pantheon of soldiers who contributed to the success of D-Day, the name of Lieutenant General Frederick Edgeworth Morgan must stand near the top of the list. It was Morgan and his staff who put together the original plan that, with modifications, that would ultimately become Operation Overlord.

Born on 5 February 1894 in Kent, England, Morgan graduated from the Royal Military College, Woolwich and was subsequently commissioned as a 2nd Lieutenant in the Royal Field Artillery in 1913. Mentioned in Dispatches twice during the World War 1, he later served in India and in the War Office.

In the 1940 Battle of France, Morgan led the support units of the 1st Armoured Division and after a lucky escape at Dunkirk, took command of I Corps District in May 1941 which had responsibility for the defense of Lincolnshire and the East Riding of Yorkshire.

In 1942, planners preparing the invasion of North Africa asked Morgan to form I Corps into a task force that could shut down any German counterattack that might put Gibraltar at risk. It was here that he first met Lieutenant General Dwight D. Eisenhower. In the end his task force was not needed, meaning Morgan was a corps commander without a corps. In January 1943, at the Casablanca Conference a decision was made to proceed with an invasion of northwest Europe sometime

in 1944. This operation, even though it had no actual commander, still needed a Chief of Staff – someone to oversee the planning – and all eyes settled on Morgan.

As Chief of Staff to the Supreme Allied Commander (COSSAC), Morgan's primary challenge was to determine where the invasion should take place. In the end, Morgan recommended Normandy as the invasion target. Once this was agreed the next issue for COSSAC was to figure out if a full-scale invasion of this area of France was feasible and realistic

Morgan's affirmative answer to that question set Overlord in motion: 'I have come to the conclusion that, in view of the limitations imposed by my directives, we may be assured of a reasonable chance of success on May 1, 1944, only if we concentrate our efforts on an assault across the Norman beaches about Bayeux,' he wrote in a 15 July 1943 cover letter to the final draft of the Overlord plan.

On 27 July the Combined Chiefs of Staff approved the COSSAC plan. However, by this time it was becoming more and more obvious that the commander of Overlord was likely to be American rather than British. With the appointment of General Eisenhower as the Supreme Commander and the setting up of SHAEF (Supreme Headquarters Allied Expeditionary Force) the COSSAC team was disbanded. Most of the staff stayed on within SHAEF in some capacity.

Eisenhower brought with him to London his current Chief of Staff Major General Walter Bedell 'Beetle' Smith, meaning there was no longer a formal place for Morgan. Despite out-ranking Smith, Morgan stayed on to help, explaining that 'I was conscious of a strong paternal feeling towards this Operation Overlord that was about to come to birth.... If, by any mischance, things went wrong, I had no illusions as to where as much as possible of the blame would be placed and I felt it would be better to be on the spot alongside those who had borne the heat and burden of the planning.'

Morgan's initial plan was enlarged to take in five landing zones, plus additional paratroopers dropping in behind the lines to help secure important strategic roads and bridges. 'There is nothing too good to say for the work he did," Eisenhower wrote in a SHAEF memo dated 9 August, 1944. "Moreover, there is no possible way of exaggerating the complexity of his task and the difficulties he had to overcome.' Morgan retired from the army in 1946 and by the time he died, on 19 March 1967, the role in which he had played in the largest seaborne invasion in history had become largely forgotten.

'There is nothing too good to say for the work he did, moreover, there is no possible way of exaggerating the complexity of his task and the difficulties he had to overcome'

General Dwight D. Eisenhower

US National Archives

Lieutenant General Frederick E. Morgan, the Chief of Staff to the Supreme Allied Commander (COSSAC).

24 Supreme Commander Dwight D. Eisenhower

Born in Denison, Texas, on 14 October 1890, Dwight David Eisenhower grew up in Abilene, Kansas, as the third of seven sons in a poor family. To the sadness of his mother, who was deeply religious, Dwight gained a position at West Point Military Academy in 1911, joining the so called 'Class the Stars Fell On'.

After graduation in 1915, Second Lieutenant Eisenhower was stationed in the US, despite several requests for an overseas posting to France. Not seeing active service in World War 1 left Eisenhower deeply disappointed, even though he was awarded the Distinguished Service Medal for his work in establishing, equipping and training the new US tank corps.

During the inter-war years the US Army went through a time of rapid expansion, and with that came swift promotions for Eisenhower and in June 1942 he was selected to be the commander of US troops in Europe. Eisenhower's rapid advancement, after a long army career spent in relative obscurity, was due not only to his knowledge of military strategy and talent for organisation but also to his ability to persuade, mediate and get along with others. Men from a wide variety of backgrounds, impressed by his friendliness, humility and persistent optimism, liked and trusted him.

After overseeing the Allied invasion of French North Africa and the amphibious assaults on Sicily and the Italian mainland Eisenhower was recalled to England and appointed Supreme Commander of the Allied Expeditionary Force (SHAEF) in January 1944. There was some surprise that President Roosevelt chose Eisenhower for this role over General Marshall, but Roosevelt felt that the former was the best politician amongst his military commanders, and so gave him the role on that basis, not necessarily because he was the best strategist.

It was a shrewd observation. Churchill was full of 'ideas,' some of which were sound, others the result of a few too many drinks. The Free French leader General Charles de Gaulle was also interfering and arrogant, acting as if he was in charge and Admiral Ernest J. King would not release landing craft from the Pacific theatre. He also had to work with some strong personalities among the military leaders he would need to work with, not least Montgomery, Patton and Leigh-Mallory.

Eisenhower was justified in his insistence on absolute unity of effort, but the final decision to launch the invasion was his and his alone.

Once the machinery of Operation Overlord had been set in motion, there was nothing more the Supreme Commander could do to affect the results. It was now down to a few thousand brave men due to wade ashore at Gold, Sword, Juno, Omaha and Utah beaches, supported by airborne landings. The accumulated experience and knowledge gleaned from the earlier landings in North Africa, Sicily and Italy, incorporated by solid staff work into a comprehensive plan, succeeded in lodging a beachhead on the continent of Europe by the late afternoon.

Once the coastal assault had succeeded, Eisenhower insisted on retaining personal control over the land battle strategy, and was immersed in the command and supply of multiple assaults through France on Germany. With three separate Army Groups vying for priority of supplies, Eisenhower had to pull of every ounce of his political savvy and leadership to address the demands of the rival commanders. In recognition of his senior position in the Allied command, he was promoted to General of the Army on 20 December 1944, equivalent to the rank of Field Marshal in most European armies.

Although he had never seen action himself, Eisenhower won the respect of front-line commanders. Having risen from Lieutenant Colonel in the Philippines to Supreme Commander of the victorious forces in Europe in only five years, Eisenhower returned home to a hero's welcome in the summer of 1945. Planned retirement was put on ice, however, when President Harry S. Truman asked him to replace General Marshall as Chief of Staff of the US Army.

US National Archives

'In preparing for battle I have always found that plans are useless, but planning is indispensable'

General Dwight D. Eisenhower gives the order of the day, 'Full victory – nothing else' to paratroopers somewhere in England, just before they board their airplanes to participate in the first assault in the invasion of the continent of Europe on 5 June 1944.

25 Air Chief Marshal Sir Arthur Tedder

Air Chief Marshal Sir Arthur Tedder was Eisenhower's deputy from December 1943 until the German surrender in May 1945. Born in Scotland on 11 July 1890, he was educated at the Whitgift School, Croydon before reading history at Magdalene College. During his last year at university he gained a reserve commission as a 2nd Lieutenant in the Dorset Regiment. With the arrival of World War 1, he was promoted to full lieutenant, but after a serious training injury he transferred to the Royal Flying Corps.

By the summer of 1916 Tedder was flying the Bristol Scout over the Western Front with No. 25 Squadron. Promotions came quickly and by the end of the war he was Squadron Leader of No. 274 Squadron, RAF – equipped with the Handley Page V/1500 bomber.

The inter-war years saw him rise through the ranks of the Royal Air Force. In November 1936, he was appointed Air Officer Commanding (AOC) RAF Far Eastern Forces, giving him command of all RAF units from Burma to Hong Kong and Borneo. The following year he returned to London to fill the new role of Director-General of research and development at the Air Ministry.

At the outbreak of war, Tedder was posted out to the Middle East where he oversaw the creation of the Western Desert air arm. As head of the RAF Middle East Command, he commanded air operations in the Mediterranean and North Africa, including the evacuation of Crete in May 1941 and Operation Crusader in North Africa later in 1941.

Although initially criticised by Churchill for underestimating the RAF resources needed to relieve Tobruk, Tedder worked tirelessly to establish good communications between ground forces and those in the air, despite the Desert Air Force being made up of an international eclectic mix of squadrons. His communication processes and strategy set the pattern for Allied air operations, not just in Africa but throughout Europe. He was promoted to Air Chief Marshal and knighted in 1942 before taking control of Mediterranean Air Command, serving under US General Dwight D. Eisenhower and getting involved in the invasions of Sicily and Tunisia.

In June 1942 after the British victory at El Alamein, Tedder enunciated ten inviolable rules of air power. These principles became the foundation upon which Allied tactical air doctrine would evolve at the Casablanca Conference in January 1943

Tedder then followed Eisenhower to SHAEF, where he became Deputy Supreme Commander. His organisation of the Allied air forces was so effective that the Luftwaffe was completely kept at bay and had little chance to interfere with the invasion. Tedder created a powerful and well co-ordinated Allied Air Force that worked well with ground forces right through France and Germany.

When the unconditional surrender of the Germans came in May 1945, Tedder signed on behalf of General Eisenhower.

After the war, Tedder was appointed Chief of Air Staff, overseeing the Berlin Airlift, before eventually retiring from the service in 1950. He died at his home in Banstead, Surrey on 3 June 1967.

Tedder's Carpet

Tedder pioneered the use of carpet-bombing as close air support for ground operations. Massive bombing was concentrated on a narrow and shallow area of the front, closely co-ordinated with advance of friendly troops. The first successful use of the technique was on 6 May 1943, at the end of the Tunisia Campaign. It was described in the press as Tedder's bomb-carpet (or Tedder's carpet). The strategy was repeated often during Operation Overlord

Alamy

Air Chief Marshal Sir Arthur Tedder on the Italian coast, December 1943.

26 Admiral Sir Bertram Ramsay

As Admiral Commander in Chief for Operation Overlord, Admiral Sir Bertram Ramsay was tasked with designing, planning and overseeing the execution of Operation Neptune. In this, he carried out what has been described by historian Correlli Barnett as a 'never surpassed masterpiece of planning'.

Born in London on 20 January 1883, the young Ramsay was educated at Colchester Royal Grammar School before joining the Royal Navy in 1898. During World War 1 he commanded a small monitor, HMS *M25* as part of the Dover Patrol – a small Royal Naval unit tasked with preventing enemy shipping, especially submarines, from entering the English Channel en route to the Atlantic. In October 1917, he took command of a larger Dover Patrol vessel, the destroyer HMS *Broke* and took part in the Second Ostend Raid and the Zeebrugge Raid, for which he was mentioned in Dispatches. Ramsay retired from the Royal Navy in 1938, but was persuaded to return by Winston Churchill in 1939. He was promoted to vice admiral and given the position of Commander in Chief, Dover on 24 August 1939, although he was still officially on the Retired List. Initially, his duties were very similar to those that he had carried out in World War 1 with the Dover Patrol, but within nine months he found himself organising the evacuation of Dunkirk and was suddenly responsible for the safe return of 338,000 men.

Working from the underground tunnels beneath Dover Castle, he and his staff worked for nine days straight to rescue the troops trapped in France by the German forces. He was knighted in recognition of the success of Operation Dynamo.

After being involved in the amphibious landings for Operation Husky (the invasion of Sicily) he returned to London in December 1943 and in April 1944 was placed back on the active list of officers with the rank of admiral. His experience of amphibious operations and his knowledge of British waters, especially the English Channel, meant he was the perfect man to orchestrate the naval aspect of Operation Overlord. In the end, Ramsay co-ordinated and commanded a fleet of almost 7,000 vessels, which delivered over 160,000 men on to the beaches of Normandy on D-Day alone. Over 875,000 disembarked by the end of June.

On 2 January 1945 Ramsay was killed when his Hudson transport aircraft crashed, soon after take-off, whilst en route to Brussels from Paris. Admiral Ramsay and four members of his staff that were aboard the plane that day are buried in Saint-Germain-en-Laye New Communal Cemetery, some ten miles west of Paris.

Before going to bed on 5 June 1944, Admiral Ramsay made a final entry in his handwritten diary:

'Thus has been made the vital and crucial decision to stage the great enterprise which (shall), I hope, be the immediate means of bringing about the downfall of Germany's fighting power and Nazi oppression and an early cessation of hostilities.

I am not under [any] delusions as to the risks involved in this most difficult of all operations.... Success will be in the balance. We must trust in our invisible assets to tip the balance in our favour. We shall require all the help that God can give us and I cannot believe that this will not be forthcoming'

Much to Ramsay's frustration, both Prime Minister Winston Churchill and King George VI declared their intentions to observe the D-Day landings from aboard HMS *Belfast.* The two were at loggerheads until meeting Ramsay, who flatly refused to take the responsibility for the safety of either figurehead. Both Churchill and the king ended up following the progress of the invasion at home

Admiral Sir Bertram Ramsay, Royal Navy (left), Naval Commander of the Normandy operation with (right), Commander Task Force 124, the Omaha Beach Assault Force onboard USS *Ancon* (AGC-4) on 25 May 1944, as preparations were underway for the invasion of France.

27 Hitler & 'The fate of the Reich'

Across the Channel, Adolf Hitler knew very well that the Allies were busy plotting an invasion of some sort or another. He just did not know where or when. During a meeting on 20 March 1944 at The Berghof, Hitler's Obersalzberg mountain retreat, the Führer addressed his Western Front Army Commanders:

It is evident that an Anglo-Saxon landing in the West will and must come. How and where it will come no one knows. Equally, no kind of speculation on the subject is possible. Whatever concentrations of shipping exist, they cannot and must not be taken as any evidence, or any indication, that the choice has fallen on any one sector of the long Western Front from Norway to the Bay of Biscay, or on the Mediterranean – the south coast of France, the Italian coast or the Balkans.

For all of his many failings, Hitler knew that the Allied top brass was not only busying itself with the planning of a large-scale invasion, but that it was also spending a great deal of time, money and effort in an attempt to mislead him and his military leaders about the where, the when, and the how of said attack. He was also under no illusion that once a landing was made, it would be 'do or die' for both sides. It really would be a pivotal battle, and perhaps decisive in foretelling which side would eventually win the war outright. Hitler was confident of repelling anything the Allies threw at him, but he was well aware of the gravity of the situation and, as he continued his address, he did not hold back his views.

Once the landing has been defeated it will under no circumstances be repeated by the enemy. Quite apart from the heavy casualties he would suffer, months would be needed for a renewed attempt. Nor is this the only factor which would deter the Anglo Americans from trying again. There would also be the crushing blow to their morale which a miscarried invasion would give.

It would, for one thing, prevent the re-election of Roosevelt in America and, with luck, he would finish up somewhere in jail. In England, too, war weariness would assert itself even more greatly than hitherto and Churchill, in view of his age and illness and with his influence on the wane, would no longer be in a position to carry through a new landing operation.

Hitler concluded his address by impressing on his commanders that, 'On every single man fighting on the Western Front … depends the outcome of the war and with it the fate of the Reich.'

Opposite Page:
Adolf Hitler walking in the snow alongside Heinrich Himmler at Berghof Berchtesgaden, 3 April 1944.

28 General Omar N. Bradley

Born in Randolph Country, Missouri on 12 February 1893, Omar Nelson Bradley worked as a boilermaker prior to gaining admission to the United States Military Academy at West Point. He was in the same class as Eisenhower and they graduated together in 1915. Bradley missed active service during World War 1, instead being tasked with guarding copper mines in Montana. After the war he returned to West Point to teach and by 1941 he was a brigadier general, commanding the Infantry School at Fort Benning.

After the US entered World War 2, Bradley oversaw the transformation of the 82nd Infantry Division into the 101st US Airborne Division. He was finally given his first front line command role during Operation Torch, some twenty-seven years after first graduating from West Point. When General Patton was re-assigned in April 1943, Bradley took command of the US II Corps for the Tunisia Campaign and the Allied invasion of Sicily. His leadership during the North African campaign led to him being promoted to Lieutenant General (three-star general) in June 1943.

In September 1943, Bradley was posted to the UK and given command of the US First Army (also known as Big Red One) who would ultimately spearhead the assault on Omaha and Utah beaches during D-Day. When he could spare the time, the General was with the troops

in field inspections, watching them run obstacle courses and engage in mortar practice. 'I will see you on the beaches,' he told the GIs.

Despite being a loyal supporter of Eisenhower, and one of the Supreme Commander's most trusted generals, Bradley was incensed when Eisenhower assigned the US First Army to Montgomery during the Ardennes offensive in December 1944 and threatened to resign. Eisenhower did not budge on his decision but to Bradley's credit he returned to the front line, remaining calm and professional in front of his men, urging them to press on in an aggressive pursuit of the disintegrating German units. On 6 April, when the Germans' defeat appeared inevitable, the general had raised the Stars and Stripes over the imposing fortress of Ehrenbreitstein, across the Rhine from Koblenz, and declared that the Germans could have no doubt about the war's outcome.

'This time we shall leave the German people with no illusions about who won the war – and no legends about who lost the war,' he said. 'They will know that the brutal Nazi creed they adopted has led them ingloriously to total defeat.'

Less than three weeks later, General Bradley linked up with Marshal Ivan Stepanovich Konev of the Soviet Union on the banks of the Elbe River on 25

April 1945, a dramatic meeting that symbolised the imminent destruction of German arms.

After Germany's capitulation, General Bradley returned to Washington and took over as head of the Veterans Administration from 1945 to 1947. He then became Chief of Staff of the Army and served two terms as chairman of the Joint Chiefs of Staff, departing in 1954. He was made a five-star general in 1950.

US Library of Congress

General Omar Bradley

'(Bradley) was a keen judge of men and their capabilities and was absolutely fair and just in his dealings with them Added to this, he was emotionally stable and possessed a grasp of the larger issues that clearly marked him for high office'

General Eisenhower

29 Field Marshal Sir Bernard Montgomery

Field Marshal Bernard Law Montgomery was one of the most prominent and successful British commanders of World War 2. Known as 'Monty', he notably commanded the Allies against General Erwin Rommel in North Africa, and in the invasions of Italy and Normandy.

Montgomery was born in Kennington, Surrey on 17 November 1887, to a Church of Ireland Minister. His upbringing was strict to say the least and undoubtedly contributed to his aloofness in later life. Montgomery attended St Paul's School and then the Royal Military College, Sandhurst, from which he was almost expelled due to rowdiness and violence. On graduation in September 1908, he was commissioned into the 1st Battalion the Royal Warwickshire Regiment as a 2nd Lieutenant.

On the outbreak of war in 1914, Montgomery found himself in the first battle of Ypres, seeing some early action at the Battle of Le Cateau and at Mons. On 13 October he took part in an Allied counterattack, where he was shot through the lung by a sniper whilst leading a bayonet charge on an enemy trench. His wound was so severe that a grave was prepared for him, however, he went on to make a full recovery. For his actions that day Montgomery was awarded the Distinguished Service Order. Between the wars he served in India, Egypt and Palestine, working his way

through the ranks to become a Brigade Commander. His outstanding leadership and planning abilities were very much appreciated, but these abilities were somewhat undermined by his abrupt and abrasive manner.

At the outbreak of World War 2, Montgomery was recalled to Europe and given command of 3rd Division, which was deployed to Belgium as part of the British Expeditionary Force. Predicting the Germans would not be stopped, he drilled his men in the art of tactical retreats. Such hard work paid off during the retreat to Dunkirk where the 3rd Division was evacuated back to Britain with minimal casualties.

After the fall of France, Montgomery was promoted to Lieutenant General and enjoyed a succession of senior appointments, but his big break came in August 1942 when, after the death of Lieutenant General William Gott, he was given the command of the British Eighth Army, which was having a rough time of it against Erwin Rommel's Afrika Korps in North Africa.

After a period of training and re-equipment the Eighth Army eventually found its feet in the desert and Montgomery delivered the first major Allied land victory of the war at El Alamein, taking over 30,000 German prisoners in the process. As a result,

Montgomery received a knighthood and became a household name back home in Britain. More importantly, he won the confidence of Churchill.

Montgomery was assigned command of 21st Army Group, which would be all of the land-based forces earmarked to take part in Operation Overlord. Eisenhower and Churchill both had reservations about working with Monty and it was only after General Sir Alan Brooke (Chief of the British Imperial General Staff) had intervened and persuaded them that he was the best man for the job that they agreed to the appointment. If it had not been for Brooke, Montgomery would have stayed in Italy.

After overseeing the meticulously-planned Rhine crossings of March 1945, Montgomery's troops advanced into Germany. He eventually accepted the surrender of all German forces in Denmark, northern Germany and the Netherlands on 4 May 1945.

After the war, Montgomery was made 1st Viscount of Alamein and appointed Commander in Chief of the British Army of the Rhine (BAOR) in Western Germany. His personal memoir, published in 1958, was particularly inflammatory. He was critical of many of his wartime colleagues, including Dwight Eisenhower, who was by then the President of the United States. He died on 24 March 1976 at his home, near Alton, Hampshire.

> ## 'In defeat, unbeatable; in victory, unbearable'
>
> **Winston Churchill**

Dogs of war

Montgomery's rivalry with Rommel was so fierce that he even named his pet spaniel after him. Monty had another dog, a fox terrier, named Hitler

Prime Minister Churchill with General Montgomery in Normandy, July 1944.

30 Major General Sir Percy Hobart

Percy Hobart was born in 1885 in Nainital, India, where his father was a civil servant. Educated at Clifton College, Bristol and the Royal Military Academy, he was posted to the elite 1st Bengal Sappers and Miners in the Indian Army after graduation and saw active service during World War 1, winning the Military Cross and the Distinguished Service Order.

After World War 1 Hobart transferred from the Royal Engineers to the Royal Tank Corps. It was in this role that he began to realise the devastating potential the tank could have in future land battles.

Hobart's ideas centred around mobility. He was convinced that the potential of his tank brigade lay in rapid and mobile deployment, not being stuck in close cooperation with slow infantry, much to the annoyance and dismay of his more conservative and orthodox superiors at the War Office. Hobart became increasingly frustrated and is quoted as saying:

Why piddle about making porridge with artillery, and then send men to drown themselves in it for a hundred yards of No Man's Land? Tanks mean advances of miles at a time, not yards!

Churchill 'Double Onion'

After several run-ins with senior staff officers, Hobart was relieved of his command in 1940, but Churchill intervened and he soon re-joined the army and was given command of 11th Armoured Division.

The attack on Dieppe in 1942 had highlighted the need for specialised and creative armour options in order to attack a fortified coastline. In March 1943, the new Chief of Imperial General Staff, General Sir Alan Brooke, offered Hobart command of the 79th (Experimental) Armoured Division with the specific intent of devising such armour for Operation Overlord. Pillboxes, mine fields, embankments, rivers and ditches would need to be overcome during the invasion and Hobart was challenged to develop the equipment and tactics to perform these tasks. To do so he improved on existing designs and created entirely new vehicles. The odd look of many of his vehicles led them to be known as 'Hobart's Funnies'.

At first, the 79th Armoured Division possessed four main types of specialist vehicle: the Duplex Drive tank (a tank that could 'swim' ashore from LSTs), the Crab (with a flail for minesweeping), the AVRE (an assault engineer tank) and the CDL (a searchlight tank). With further development more vehicles were added to Hobart's garage, including the Crocodile (a flame-throwing Churchill tank), the Buffalo (an armoured amphibious vehicle) and the Kangaroo (an armoured personnel carrier).

These peculiar-looking vehicles proved their worth in supporting ground troops in heavily defended territory and helped the invasion become a resounding success. For the rest of the war in Europe Hobart's Funnies were constantly called upon by both British and American commanders to solve otherwise impossible problems.

The Churchill flail tanks, flamethrower tanks, and AVREs were particularly useful against German fortifications, but all of the 'funnies' regularly demonstrated their ability to cross terrain that was impassable to other Allied tanks, carry out specialist jobs that no other vehicle could undertake and accept punishment that other tanks could not face. Hobart's units became the go-to 'trouble-shooters' for almost everyone.

Hobart's Funnies

The majority of the designs were modified versions of the Churchill tank or the Sherman tank. Among the many specialist vehicles were:

Crocodile: a Churchill tank modified by the fitting of a flame-thrower in place of the hull machine-gun. It proved highly effective at clearing bunkers, trenches and other German fortifications

AVRE (Assault Vehicle Royal Engineers): a Churchill tank adapted to attack German defensive fortifications. The AVRE's main gun was replaced by a petard mortar that fired a 40 lb (18 kg) HE-filled projectile (nicknamed the 'flying dustbin') 150 yards (137 m); it was capable of destroying concrete obstacles such as roadblocks and bunkers

ARK (Armoured Ramp Carrier): a Churchill tank without a turret that had extendable ramps at each end, other vehicles could drive up ramps and over the vehicle to scale obstacles

Crab: a modified Sherman tank equipped with a mine flail, a rotating cylinder of weighted chains that exploded mines in the path of the tank

DD or 'Duplex Drive' tank: a converted M4A1 or M4A4 Sherman or Valentine tank fitted with a large watertight canvas skirting and propellers which enabled the tank to 'swim' towards shore and give close armour support to assault troops

31 President Roosevelt's D-Day Prayer

On 6 June 1944, on live radio, US President Franklin Roosevelt went on national radio to address the nation for the first time about the Normandy invasion. His speech took the form of a prayer.

The date and timing of the Normandy invasion had of course been top secret. During the previous day's broadcast on about the Allied liberation of Rome, President Roosevelt made no mention of the Normandy operation, already underway at that time.

Knowing the terrible odds facing American forces as they crossed the channel and on to open beaches under heavy enemy fire, President Roosevelt beseeched God on behalf of an anxious nation in one of the largest mass prayers in history.

My fellow Americans: Last night, when I spoke with you about the fall of Rome, I knew at that moment that troops of the United States and our allies were crossing the Channel in another and greater operation. It has come to pass with success thus far.

And so, in this poignant hour, I ask you to join with me in prayer:

Almighty God: Our sons, pride of our Nation, this day have set upon a mighty endeavor, a struggle to preserve our Republic, our religion, and our civilization, and to set free a suffering humanity.

Lead them straight and true; give strength to their arms, stoutness to their hearts, steadfastness in their faith.

They will need Thy blessings. Their road will be long and hard. For the enemy is strong. He may hurl back our forces. Success may not come with rushing speed, but we shall return again and again; and we know that by Thy grace, and by the righteousness of our cause, our sons will triumph.

They will be sore tried, by night and by day, without rest - until the victory is won. The darkness will be rent by noise and flame. Men's souls will be shaken with the violences of war.

For these men are lately drawn from the ways of peace. They fight not for the lust of conquest. They fight to end conquest. They fight to liberate. They fight to let justice arise, and tolerance and good will among all Thy people. They yearn but for the end of battle, for their return to the haven of home. Some will never return. Embrace these, Father, and receive them, Thy heroic servants, into Thy kingdom.

And for us at home - fathers, mothers, children, wives, sisters, and brothers of brave men overseas - whose thoughts and prayers are ever with them - help us, Almighty God, to rededicate ourselves in renewed faith in Thee in this hour of great sacrifice.

Many people have urged that I call the nation into a single day of special prayer. But because the road is long and the desire is great, I ask that our people devote themselves in a continuance of prayer. As we rise to each new day, and again when each day is spent, let words of prayer be on our lips, invoking Thy help to our efforts.

Give us strength, too - strength in our daily tasks, to redouble the contributions we make in the physical and the material support of our armed forces.

And let our hearts be stout, to wait out the long travail, to bear sorrows that may come, to impart our courage unto our sons wheresoever they may be.

And, O Lord, give us Faith. Give us Faith in Thee; Faith in our sons; Faith in each other; Faith in our united crusade. Let not the keenness of our spirit ever be dulled. Let not the impacts of temporary events, of temporal matters of but fleeting moment - let not these deter us in our unconquerable purpose.

With Thy blessing, we shall prevail over the unholy forces of our enemy. Help us to conquer the apostles of greed and racial arrogancies. Lead us to the saving of our country, and with our sister nations into a world unity that will spell a sure peace - a peace invulnerable to the schemings of unworthy men. And a peace that will let all of men live in freedom, reaping the just rewards of their honest toil.

Thy will be done, Almighty God.
Amen.

32 The Weather

On 8 May the final date for D-Day was formally set by General Eisenhower. The invasion was set for 5 June 1944.

As May gave way to June thousands of assault troops emerged from barracks, tent cities and secure compounds across England and marched through towns and villages on their way to their embarkation sites. The first tentative moves of the invasion were taking place but ultimately there was only one man who could press the 'go' button and that was Eisenhower. His was a difficult decision and could be ruined by one vital factor beyond his control. The weather.

On 29 May the senior meteorologist for SHAEF, Group Captain J.M. Stagg of the RAF, had drawn up a long-range forecast that suggested the first week of June would be suitable weather-wise for the invasion. From 1 June the Commanders in Chief met each other twice a day to pour over detailed weather reports.

Meanwhile, the Germans were also keenly watching the weather. On 3 June Rommel wrote in his daily report:

Concentrated air attacks on the coastal defences between Dunkirk and Dieppe and on the ports strengthen the supposition that the main invasion effort will be made in that area.... Since 1 June an increasing number of warning messages has been broadcast to the French Resistance....

The weather had started to deteriorate significantly by this time and in Rommel's eyes the threat of imminent invasion seemed minimal. German naval experts were convinced the Allies needed five clear days to launch an invasion, so Rommel took the opportunity to head home to see his wife and to ask Hitler to release some panzer resources before the attack came.

Back at SHAEF, 3 June was a day of intense anxiety. Group Captain Stagg met the Supreme Commander and his staff – he had bad news. The period of settled weather they had been enjoying had come to an abrupt end and the new forecast for 5 June was showing storms, high winds and low cloud. After discussions it was decided, however, to let the invasion force continue their preparations – at least for the time being.

The final weather conference was scheduled for 04:00 on 4 June. Convoys were forming up in open seas and final preparations were being made. The weather forecast for 5 June was bad; stormy and overcast with a cloud base of 500 ft and force 5 winds. Even worse was that the weather was deteriorating so quickly that accurate forecasts for more that twenty-four hours in advance were almost impossible.

It was the cloud cover that worried Eisenhower the most. With low cloud it would be difficult, if not impossible, to provide either air or naval support to the invasion beaches. Ultimately, Eisenhower was not willing to risk an invasion without the requisite back-up and decided to put everything on hold for twenty-four hours. A prearranged signal was sent out to the invasion fleet, many of which were already at sea.

Another weather meeting took place that evening. This time Group Captain Stagg offered up a glimmer of hope. He anticipated a break in the storm, a window of thirty-six hours of relatively clear weather that offered an enticing opportunity to proceed. Eisenhower canvassed opinion from the rest of SHAEF; the next available date with favourable tidal conditions was 19 June, although there would be no moon to aid the airbourne assault. Then there was the question of morale and security. SHAEF was divided as to go ahead or not.

The discussions continued, General Eisenhower went around the room asking opinions. There was no outright consensus. He paced the meeting room in silence, all eyes following him. At 21:45 he gave his decision. 'I am quite positive we must give the order.'

By 23:00 every vessel involved in the invasion had been given the order to resume operations. D-Day would be 6 June 1944.

Eisenhower went back to his trailer to grab a few hours' sleep. He was back at Southwick House again in the early hours of the morning for the final weather meeting – a storm was raging outside, with gale force winds and horizontal rain, but as Stagg entered the room he had a grin on his face – he was even more certain than the previous evening that the weather would break in time for the planned invasion, but it would only be good for Tuesday 6. By Wednesday the weather would be rough once more.

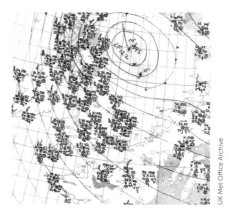

UK Met Office Archive

Forecaster's surface chart for 1300 GMT on 6 June 1944 when troops had been landing since dawn.

The invasion fleet was sailing into the Channel; if they were to call it all off, it had to be done now and the Supreme Commander was the only person capable of calling the shots. He paced once more, deliberating for what, for some, seemed like an eternity. Finally, he stopped pacing, turned to face his audience and said, 'OK, we'll go.'

Cheers rang out through Southwick House.

33 General Eisenhower's Order of the Day

On the evening of 5 June 1944, just hours prior to the D-Day landings in Normandy, copies of General Eisenhower's Order of the Day were distributed to members of the Allied forces. The meticulously crafted, motivational call-to-arms was drafted by Eisenhower himself over a period of several months and was distributed to the 175,000-strong invasion force as it went through its final preparations for the operation.

The moment the men received and read the leaflet must have been an intense one. Thousands of men crowded on ships in the middle of the ocean, or on airfields in southern England readying themselves for the attack. A moment of quiet as every man took in the words of encouragement from their leader. A moment of realisation that they were about to take part in the greatest and most important invasion in the history of invasions.

In this one moment it all became real.

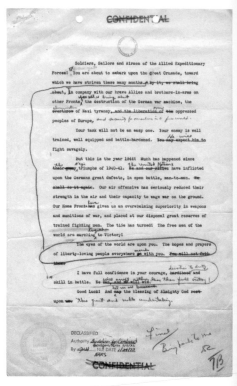

Eisenhower's draft message.

SUPREME HEADQUARTERS
ALLIED EXPEDITIONARY FORCE

Soldiers, Sailors and Airmen of the Allied Expeditionary Force!

You are about to embark upon the Great Crusade, toward which we have striven these many months. The eyes of the world are upon you. The hopes and prayers of liberty-loving people everywhere march with you. In company with our brave Allies and brothers-in-arms on other Fronts, you will bring about the destruction of the German war machine, the elimination of Nazi tyranny over the oppressed peoples of Europe, and security for ourselves in a free world.

Your task will not be an easy one. Your enemy is well trained, well equipped and battle-hardened. He will fight savagely.

But this is the year 1944! Much has happened since the Nazi triumphs of 1940-41. The United Nations have inflicted upon the Germans great defeats, in open battle, man-to-man. Our air offensive has seriously reduced their strength in the air and their capacity to wage war on the ground. Our Home Fronts have given us an overwhelming superiority in weapons and munitions of war, and placed at our disposal great reserves of trained fighting men. The tide has turned! The free men of the world are marching together to Victory!

I have full confidence in your courage, devotion to duty and skill in battle. We will accept nothing less than full Victory!

Good Luck! And let us all beseech the blessing of Almighty God upon this great and noble undertaking.

Dwight D Eisenhower

34 Operation Neptune – Special Order of the Day

With almost 7,000 ships disembarking over 130,000 men, plus artillery, tanks, vehicles and supplies across five landing area, Operation Neptune was the largest maritime invasion in history.

The Royal Navy's role in Operation Neptune is well summarised in Admiral Ramsay's special order of the day which was communicated out to all the Allied naval forces under his command a week before the invasion took place:

SPECIAL ORDER OF THE DAY TO THE OFFICERS AND MEN OF THE ALLIED NAVAL EXPEDITIONARY FORCE.

It is to be our privilege to take part in the greatest amphibious operation in history—a necessary preliminary to the opening of the Western Front in Europe which in conjunction with the great Russian advance, will crush the fighting power of Germany.

This is the opportunity which we have long awaited and which must be seized and pursued with relentless determination : the hopes and prayers of the free world and of the enslaved peoples of Europe will be with us and we cannot fail them.

Our task in conjunction with the Merchant Navies of the United Nations, and supported by the Allied Air Forces, is to carry the Allied Expeditionary Force to the Continent, to establish it there in a secure bridgehead and to build it up and maintain it at a rate which will outmatch that of the enemy.

Let no one underestimate the magnitude of this task.

The Germans are desperate and will resist fiercely until we out-manœuvre and out-fight them, which we can and we will do. To every one of you will be given the opportunity to show by his determination and resource that dauntless spirit of resolution which individually strengthens and inspires and which collectively is irresistible.

I count on every man to do his utmost to ensure the success of this great enterprise which is the climax of the European war.

Good luck to you all and God speed.

B. H. Ramsay

ADMIRAL.
ALLIED NAVAL COMMANDER-IN-CHIEF,
EXPEDITIONARY FORCE.

35 In case of failure

With such a massive operation, there was bound to be a tiny element of doubt in Eisenhower's mind as he sent his men into battle against a well prepared and highly organised enemy. What would happen if the invasion floundered on the beaches? If the Allies did not secure a strong foothold on D-Day, they would be ordered into a full retreat, and he would be forced to make public a message he had drafted for such an occasion.

The transcript of the short message (mistakenly dated 5 July) reads:

Our landings in the Cherbourg-Havre area have failed to gain a satisfactory foothold and I have withdrawn the troops. My decision to attack at this time and place was based upon the best information available. The troops, the air and the navy did all that bravery and devotion to duty could do. If any blame or fault attaches to the attempt it is mine alone.

Fortunately, the note was not needed. However it was kept by Eisenhower's naval aide, Captain Harry C. Butcher, otherwise we may never had known of its existence.

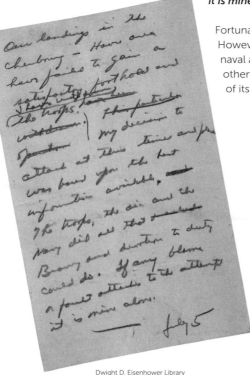

Dwight D. Eisenhower Library

36 Monty's message

It was customary that prior to sending his men into battle, Field Marshal Montgomery issued them all with a personal message. The reasons behind doing this were numerous: Montgomery believed that by giving each man the same, clear message it would help define the overall objective of why they were fighting and thereby instil a strong sense of purpose amongst the men. His letters also did much to build the spirit of the soldiers and strengthen their will to win.

On the eve of D-Day, the following message was issued to the Commonwealth units involved in the invasion, with the explicit order that it be read aloud to all troops.

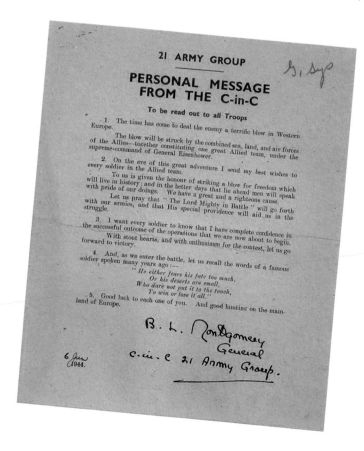

37 Lt. General Crerar's D-Day message

Lieutenant General H.D.G. Crerar was the Commanding Officer of the First Canadian Army and, just like Field Marshal Montgomery, he too felt the need to write a personal message to each and every Canadian soldier that would be taking part in the Normandy invasion. (He was promoted in full general in November 1944).

Below is the short message, which was read out to all Canadian units on the eve of the attack.

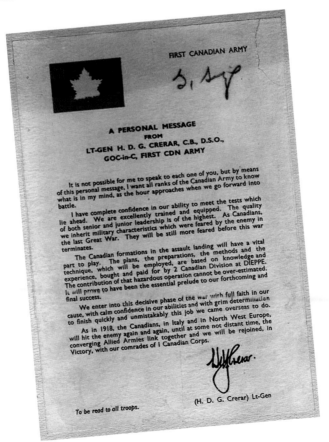

FIRST CANADIAN ARMY

A PERSONAL MESSAGE
FROM
LT-GEN H. D. G. CRERAR, C.B., D.S.O.,
GOC-in-C, FIRST CDN ARMY

It is not possible for me to speak to each one of you, but by means of this personal message, I want all ranks of the Canadian Army to know what is in my mind, as the hour approaches when we go forward into battle.

I have complete confidence in our ability to meet the tests which lie ahead. We are excellently trained and equipped. The quality of both senior and junior leadership is of the highest. As Canadians, we inherit military characteristics which were feared by the enemy in the last Great War. They will be still more feared before this war terminates.

The Canadian formations in the assault landing will have a vital part to play. The plans, the preparations, the methods and the technique, which will be employed, are based on knowledge and experience, bought and paid for by 2 Canadian Division at DIEPPE. The contribution of that hazardous operation cannot be over-estimated. It will prove to have been the essential prelude to our forthcoming and final success.

We enter into this decisive phase of the war with full faith in our cause, with calm confidence in our abilities and with grim determination to finish quickly and unmistakably this job we came overseas to do.

As in 1918, the Canadians, in Italy and in North West Europe, will hit the enemy again and again, until at some not distant time, the converging Allied Armies link together and we will be rejoined, in Victory, with our comrades of I Canadian Corps.

(H. D. G. Crerar) Lt-Gen

To be read to all troops.

38 Eisenhower's broadcast to Europe

As the morning of the invasion progressed and beachheads formed on almost all the landing zones, Supreme Commander Eisenhower saw fit to deliver a radio address to the people of Western Europe.

Read by his press aide, Colonel Ernest Dupuy, it was designed to assure them that their hour of liberation was coming ever closer.

It was 09:32 London time.

WikiCommons

Portrait of General Eisenhower

People of Western Europe: A landing was made this morning on the coast
of France by troops of the Allied Expeditionary Force. This landing
is part of the concerted United Nations plan for the liberation of
Europe, made in conjunction with our great Russian allies.

I have this message for all of you. Although the initial assault may
not have been made in your own country, the hour of your liberation is
approaching.

All patriots, men and women, young and old, have a part to play in
the achievement of final victory. To members of resistance movements,
I say, follow the instructions you have received. To patriots who
are not members of organized resistance groups, I say, continue your
passive resistance, but do not needlessly endanger your lives until
I give you the signal to rise and strike the enemy. The day will come
when I shall need your united strength. Until that day, I call on you
for the hard task of discipline and restraint.

Citizens of France! I am proud to have again under my command the
gallant Forces of France. Fighting beside their Allies, they will play
a worthy part in the liberation of their Homeland.

Because the initial landing has been made on the soil of your country,
I repeat to you with even greater emphasis my message to the peoples
of other occupied countries in Western Europe. Follow the instructions
of your leaders. A premature uprising of all Frenchmen may prevent you
from being of maximum help to your country in the critical hour. Be
patient. Prepare!

As Supreme Commander of the Allied Expeditionary Force, there is
imposed on me the duty and responsibility of taking all measures
necessary to the prosecution of the war. Prompt and willing obedience
to the orders that I shall issue is essential.

Effective civil administration of France must be provided by
Frenchmen. All persons must continue in their present duties unless
otherwise instructed. Those who have made common cause with the enemy
and so betrayed their country will be removed. As France is liberated
from her oppressors, you yourselves will choose your representatives,
and the government under which you wish to live.

In the course of this campaign for the final defeat of the enemy you
may sustain further loss and damage. Tragic though they may be, they
are part of the price of victory. I assure you that I shall do all
in my power to mitigate your hardships. I know that I can count on
your steadfastness now, no less than in the past. The heroic deeds of
Frenchmen who have continued the struggle against the Nazis and their
Vichy satellites, in France and throughout the French Empire, have
been an example and an inspiration to all of us.

This landing is but the opening phase of the campaign in Western
Europe. Great battles lie ahead. I call upon all who love freedom
to stand with us. Keep your faith staunch — our arms are resolute —
together we shall achieve victory.

39 Major John Howard

Born into a working-class family in London's West End, Reginald John Howard was not your typical British Army officer candidate. However, he rose through the ranks to lead perhaps one of the most celebrated operations in modern British military history – the spectacular airborne assault on the two bridges over the River Orne and the Caen Canal – better known as Pegasus Bridge. Howard was born on 8 December 1912, the eldest of nine children. He excelled at school but his family's financial situation forced him to find work at fourteen. He worked as a clerk in a local brokerage firm, taking evening classes to further his learning, but in 1931 the brokerage firm went out of business and Howard found himself out of work.

Howard joined the army and served for six years in the King's Shropshire Light Infantry, before leaving after the completion of his six year enlistment period to join the Oxford City Police. His stint as a policeman was short-lived, however, as he re-joined his old regiment in December 1939 after the outbreak of war. Within six months he was put on an officers' training course and on 9 November 1940 he was commissioned as a 2nd Lieutenant with 2nd Battalion, Oxfordshire and Buckinghamshire Light Infantry.

In 1941 Howard was promoted to Captain. Towards the end of that year news filtered through to Howard that his battalion was to be converted into a glider-borne unit and become a part of the newly formed 1st Airlanding Brigade. Howard was very enthusiastic at the prospect of this exciting new role, and took his responsibility as a commander very seriously indeed, so much so that, for the most part, he abstained from drinking in order to keep a clear mind.

During the planning phases for the D-Day landings, Major General 'Windy' Gale had decided on a glider-borne raid to capture the Bénouville and Ranville bridges and after a three-day proving exercise Lieutenant Colonel Roberts invited Howard into his office and told him that 'D' Company had been chosen to spearhead the entire British invasion effort.

Invasion planning continued apace. Besides Howard, no one in the Company had any idea why they were constantly working on the art of capturing bridges and, frankly, everyone was getting a little bored by it. Howard took his men to one side and assured them in as plainly as he could, 'We are training for some special purpose. You'll find a lot of the training that we are doing, this capturing of things like bridges, is connected with that special purpose. If any of you mention the word "bridges" outside our training hours and I get to know about it, you'll be for the high jump and your feet won't touch before you are RTU [Returned To Unit].'

At 11:00 on 5 June 1944, Six Horsa gliders took off from Tarrant Rushton in Dorset, carrying Major Howard and 179 men of the Ox and Bucks Light Infantry. At 00:07 the lead glider passed over the French coast at about 6,000 ft, cut its ties to their bomber escort and started its descent towards the bridges. In what can only be described as an extraordinary feat of flying, the lead glider had landed just feet from the target. What is more, the enemy had not been alerted. Within 15 minutes of landing, both bridges were in British hands and, more importantly, still intact.

In September 1944, 'D' Company returned to England for some well-earned leave. Out of the 180 men who had taken part in the original D-Day raid on Pegasus Bridge, only forty remained. Once back in England Howard set about the task of re-building the Company, however a serious road accident in November that year saw him break both legs, his left knee and his right hip. He was hospitalised until March 1945 and played no further part in the war. Eventually he was invalided out of the army altogether. After the war Howard worked for the National Savings Committee and the Ministry for Agriculture, before retiring in 1974. He died on 5 May 1999, aged 86.

Major John Howard, DSO

Bronze bust memorial statue of Major John Howard at Pegasus Bridge, Bénouville, Normandy.

Alamy

The Longest Day

Howard's experiences on D-Day were re-enacted by actor Richard Todd in the film *The Longest Day*. Todd had actually taken part in D-Day himself, serving in the 7th Parachute Battalion

40 Robert Capa - The Magnificent Eleven

Robert Capa was a Hungarian combat photographer who, after moving from Berlin to Paris to avoid the Nazis, made a name for himself by covering the Spanish Civil War with journalist and author Ernest Hemmingway – a journey later described in Hemmingway's *For Whom The Bell Tolls* and published in *Life* magazine..

When it came to the D-Day invasion, Robert Capa was the only press photographer who managed to go in with the first wave of infantry. According to the account first given in *Life* magazine, he landed at dawn with E Company, 2nd Battalion of the 16th Regiment, 1st US Infantry Division on the 'Easy Red' sector of the beach code-named Omaha. Capa later recalled the moment his landing craft hit the beach:

My beautiful France looked sordid and uninviting, and a German machine-gun, spitting bullets around the barge, fully spoiled my return. The men from my barge waded in the water. Waist-deep, with rifles ready to shoot, with the invasion obstacles and the smoking beach in the background.

Ducking and diving behind obstacles, Capa somehow managed to shoot four rolls of film – over one hundred pictures – within the first two hours of the invasion. After feeling that he had pushed his luck as far as he could on the beach that morning, he headed back to England on a hospital ship full of wounded to hand in his films.

John G. Morris, a London based editor at *Life* magazine received a call at about 18:00 on Wednesday 7 June saying the Capa's films were on their way to him. Hours later a motorcycle messenger arrived with a small packet of films accompanied by a short, handwritten note; 'John, all the action is in the four rolls of 35 mm.'

Morris immediately got the films across to the *Life* darkroom, telling them to rush – he was desperate not to miss the evening deadline and he needed four of each negative in order to pass censorship checks.

'I was surprised to see him there. I saw the press badge and I thought, "What the hell is he doing here?" He helped me out of the water and then he took off down the beach for some more photos'

Huston Riley

Some of those famous images published in Life ran with captions that described the footage as 'slightly out of focus', explaining that Capa's hands were shaking in the excitement of the moment (something that he denied). Capa used this phrase as the title of his autobiographical account of the war:

American Troops Landing on D-Day, Omaha Beach, Normandy Coast, France.

A few minutes later a lad from the darkroom rushed, into the office of Morris screaming, 'The films are ruined. Ruined!' He explained that he had hung them in the locker that served as a drying cabinet, which was normal practice, but because of the rush he had closed the doors. Consequently, there was too much heat in the room and the emulsion melted. Only eleven images were useable, the rest were useless.

Those eleven images became known as 'The Magnificent Eleven' and are the images that made the lead story in *Life* magazine on 19 June, 1944: 'BEACHHEADS OF NORMANDY: The Fateful Battle for Europe is Joined by Sea and Air.' These are undoubtably the images by which many now remember D-Day: 6 June, 1944.

Experts have recently begun to debate the story behind photojournalism's most potent and durable myth, questioning water damage to equipment, photographic materials and darkroom practices. Evidence also suggests Capa was not part of the first wave and exposes inaccurate captions with the photographs

41 Lord Lovat

Throughout the entirety of World War 2, Lord Lovat saw no more than six days of action, yet he has become renowned as a true war hero.

Simon Christopher Joseph Fraser was born on 9 July 1911 at Beaufort Castle, Inverness, Scotland, the son of the 14th Lord Lovat. After graduating from Magdalen College, Oxford, he was commissioned as a 2nd Lieutenant in the Lovat Scouts (a Scottish territorial infantry regiment formed by his father in 1900 for service in the Second Boer War), although he transferred to the regular army a year later, joining the Scots Guards.

His father died in 1933, leaving him the title of 25th Chief of the Clan Fraser Lovat and an estate in Inverness amounting to nearly 200,000 acres. He was just twenty-two.

Lord Lovat left the army in 1937 in order to take over the running of the family estate but less than a year later, with war approaching, he returned as a Captain in his old regiment, the Lovat Scouts. In 1940 he volunteered to join one of the new commando units being formed by the British Army, and was eventually attached to No. 4 Commando. On 3 March 1941, Nos 3 and 4 Commando launched a successful raid on the German-occupied Norwegian Lofoten Islands, destroying fish-oil factories, petrol dumps, and eleven ships. They also seized encryption equipment and codebooks and captured over 200 German prisoners.

A month later, Lord Lovat found himself commanding a raid on the French coastal village of Hardelot, for which he was awarded the Military Cross. By 1942 Lord Lovat had been promoted to acting Lieutenant Colonel and was now the commanding officer of No. 4 Commando – his next piece of the action would be as part of the disastrous Dieppe raid on 19 August 1942 where the performance of his commandos was a rare highlight that owed much to Lovat's meticulous pre-planning. As a result, Lovat was awarded the Distinguished Service Order.

When the planning for Operation Overlord started, it was quickly apparent that a large number of commando forces would be needed to operate under a single command, so Lovat was promoted to Brigadier and given charge of the 1st Special Service Brigade.

When the brigade began its preparation for the D-Day landings, he devoted himself almost entirely to training. Lovat was no conventional regular soldier. Indeed, he was quite the opposite, but he knew how to build and motivate a group of men. He was demanding, he trained his men intensely and he was completely intolerant of inefficiency. However, his methods worked and when eventually his Commando Brigade landed on Sword Red Beach, it was probably as perfect a fighting force as could be found anywhere.

Lovat's 1st Special Service Brigade waded ashore as part of the second assault wave on Sword Beach, played on to the sand by Lovat's personal piper, Bill Millin. Once off the sand, Lovat's men pressed on towards the Orne bridges to support the British 6th Airborne Division, arriving just one hour later than planned, for which Lord Lovat apologised to the waiting Lieutenant Colonel Richard Pine-Coffin. Lovat's war ended prematurely on 12 June, during the Battle of Breville, when he was seriously wounded by an exploding shell whilst observing an artillery bombardment.

After the war Lord Lovat joined the government as Parliamentary Under-Secretary of State for Foreign Affairs but he resigned this position when Winston Churchill lost the subsequent election. Regardless, Lord Lovat's involvement in politics would continue for the next forty-two years both in the House of Lords and as a member of the Inverness County Council.

Lord Lovat died on 16 March 1995, aged 83. Bill Millin, who had piped the Commandos ashore on D-Day, played at his funeral.

'He [Lovat] was in a frightful mess; a large shell fragment had cut deeply into his back and side: Peter Tasker, No. 6 Commando's medical officer, was giving a blood transfusion. He was very calm. "Take over the brigade," he said, "and whatever happens – not a foot back." He repeated this several times. And then, "Get me a priest," he said. "Get me the Abbé de Naurois"'

Lieutenant-Colonel Derek Mills-Roberts

The Lord Lovat, CO of No. 4 Commando, at Newhaven after returning from the Dieppe Raid (Operation Jubilee), August 1942.

42 Piper Bill Millin

At approximately 08:40 on D-Day, Bill Millin disembarked from his landing craft and headed for Sword Beach. He was just a few metres behind his commanding officer, Brigadier Lord Lovat, commander of 1st Special Service Brigade. At the beginning of their adventure, as their landing craft set sail from the River Hamble, Lovat informed Millin that he wanted him to play his pipes as the men went ashore, despite the War Office banning the playing of pipes during D-Day in case they attracted unwanted enemy fire. 'Ah, but that's the English War Office, Millin,' Lovat told him. 'You and I are both Scottish, so that doesn't apply.'

As Millin jumped into the icy water and the Cameron clan tartan of his kilt billowed and floated to the surface, he launched into one of Lovat's favourite tunes, Hielan' Laddie. Lovat, firing his old Winchester rifle and brandishing a walking stick, turned around and gave Millin a thumbs-up. Millin continued to play as he waded ashore. He did not waver, even though he had to walk past numerous men from his detachment floating face down in the surf.

Once ashore Millin carried on playing, walking up and down the beach in the heat of the battle, playing tune after tune. Many of the men were appreciative of the pipes; the tunes gave them a much-needed morale boost as they frantically tried to find shelter away from enemy fire. Eventually, Millin's brigade moved off

towards Bénouville where they had orders to join up with Major John Howard and his men who had captured a nearby bridge (later known as Pegasus bridge) in the small hours of the morning. As the men moved away from Sword Beach, Millin was at the front, piping them along the road. On their arrival at Bénouville, the Commandos came under intense fire. Millin walked calmly at the head of the column playing Blue Bonnets with the rest of the commandos following him down the main street.

When they eventually came to Bénouville bridge, troops on the other side of the canal signalled frantically that it was under sniper fire. Lovat ordered Millin to shoulder his bagpipes once more and so to the sound of Millin's pipes, the commandos marched across Pegasus bridge.

Millin's pipes were hit by shrapnel and damaged a few days after the D-Day landings and he had another set sent out to him. The original set of pipes are now on display in Dawlish Museum, along with his kilt, bonnet and dirk.

After being demobbed in 1946, Millin took a job on Lord Lovat's highland estate, before training as a psychiatric nurse. Millin's exploits on D-Day were immortalised in the 1962 film The Longest Day, with Millin played by Pipe Major Leslie de Laspee who was the official piper to the Queen Mother at the time. Millin died in August 2010.

Landing on Queen Red Beach, Sword. Millin is in the foreground at the right; Lovat is wading through the water to the right of the column.

'When they heard the pipes, some of the lads started cheering but one wasn't very pleased, and he called me "the mad bastard". Well, we usually referred to Lovat as the mad bastard, but this was the first time I had heard it referred to me'

Bill Millin

Although his exploits did not earn him a British gallantry medal, Piper Millin was awarded the highest order of merit in France, the Légion d'honneur, in June 2009

43 Sergeant Major Stanley Hollis VC

Middlesbrough-born Stanley Hollis was the only man to win the Victoria Cross (VC) on D-Day. By the time of the invasion he was only in his early thirties but in four years of fighting with the Green Howards (Yorkshire Regiment) he had already seen action at Dunkirk, in the African desert against the elite Afrika Korps and in Sicily. He was a tough and wily veteran who had been seriously wounded several times in action, deserved his promotions and had forged a reputation as something of cult hero amongst his men.

The battle-hardened Green Howards were handpicked by Field Marshal Montgomery to capture and disarm the Mont Fleury Battery, a network of concrete strongpoints boasting enough firepower to put a severe dent in the Gold Beach landings. The battery was heavily fortified with thick belts of barbed wire, deep minefields and multiple machine-gun nests. It was a difficult and dangerous job, and heavy casualties were expected. As the ramps went down and the first wave of attackers waded ashore the men were dangerously exposed and vulnerable, and Hollis did his best to encourage his men to keep moving and get away from the 'killing zone' of the sea surf. When they reached the top of the beach, sappers from the Royal Engineers started to clear a path through the minefield that led up to the Mont Fleury Battery. Once a path had been cleared and marked out with white tape, an advance party scrambled forward, but they were soon pinned down by machine-gun fire.

After taking a few minutes to locate the offending enemy pill-box, Hollis took his Sten gun, clambered up onto his feet and charged at the enemy. As he sprinted forward, weaving and ducking as he went, he fired his gun from the hip at the fortified strongpoint. The German gunners retaliated in kind, grazing his ear and his eyebrow, but they failed to stop him. In a matter of seconds Hollis was on top of the concrete roof of the pill-box and priming a grenade, which he dropped through the gun slit. After a muffled explosion the German survivors staggered outside where Hollis promptly took them all prisoner.

As he was organising his new-found friends, Hollis spotted a trench running out towards another bunker. Hollis slapped a fresh magazine into his Sten and rushed the second strongpoint. Thinking that they had been outflanked by a strong enemy attack, the men inside the bunker surrendered with no trouble. In a matter of minutes, Hollis had single-handedly neutralised two enemy pill-boxes and taken dozens of prisoners, clearing the way for his men to seize the Mont Fleury Battery. It was an incredible piece of bravery and action, and for it he was recommended for the Victoria Cross.

However, Hollis was not quite done for the day. By noon, Gold Beach had been made safe and the Green Howards were moving inland. Hollis and his platoon had been ordered to reconnoitre the village of Crépon and clear a path through it for the rest of the battalion. After spotting an enemy artillery position beyond a remote farmhouse, he reported his findings to a senior officer, Major Lofthouse, and promptly returned to the farmhouse with a PIAT and a couple of machine-gunners. Unfortunately, Hollis missed with the PIAT, and immediately all three men came under intense fire. Hollis ordered a retreat and managed to crawl out of the field and get back to relative safety, but his two machine-gunners became trapped in a field with the enemy rapidly closing in on them.

Major Lofthouse turned to Hollis and informed him, 'Those are your men, Sergeant Major.'

'I know sir,' Hollis answered. 'And as it was me who took them in, I'll be the one to bring them out.'

On his return to the farmhouse, he could see the Germans walking through the field, firing their machine-guns in an effort to flush out the two Green Howards – it was only a matter of minutes before they were discovered.

Hollis waded into the field, firing his Bren, calling out to his men. Under his covering fire the two soldiers got to their feet and ran to the safety of the farmhouse. Once they were out of danger, Hollis followed them. Now he was the subject of concentrated enemy fire and only just managed to get back himself after a hair-raising dash across the open field.

Due to another act of bravery worthy of a VC, Hollis had successfully managed to get his men out of a seemingly hopeless situation unhurt.

In September 1944 Hollis was badly injured by a German mortar shell. It was while he was recovering in hospital in England that he heard he had won the Victoria Cross. He was officially invested by King George VI at Buckingham Palace the following month. Although he carried out two actions worthy of the Victoria Cross on D-Day, army rules stipulate that subsequent VC awards will only be considered if they took place on different days. Because both actions took place on 6 June 1944, he could only be awarded a single VC.

44 Violette Szabo GC

One of the bravest women of the war, Violette Szabo joined the Special Operations Executive (SOE) in order to avenge the death of her husband who was killed at El Alamein in October 1942. She was parachuted into France forty-eight hours after D-Day to help the Resistance but was captured, tortured and executed by the Germans in 1944, aged just twenty-three.

Violette and her husband Étienne.

Violette was born in Paris on 26 June 1921 to an English father and a French mother. Despite the family moving to England soon after her birth, Violette spent a lot of time in France and grew up to be fluent in both French and English. In 1940, Violette joined the Land Army picking fruit and then worked in an armament factory in London. In the same year she met and married thirty-one-year-old Étienne Szabo, a dashing French Foreign Legionnaire. She was just nineteen. In June 1942, just four months after the birth of their daughter, Tania, Étienne was killed during the Second Battle of El Alamein in North Africa.

Violette was devastated by the news and vowed to avenge his death. She applied for a role in the Special Operations Executive – her fluent French was a big advantage and, after undergoing gruelling training, she was recruited into the 'F' Section of the SOE. She was handed her first mission in April 1944 – she was to travel alone to Rouen and Le Havre to establish the fate of a Resistance group thought to have been infiltrated by the Germans. It was an incredibly dangerous mission but, despite being arrested twice she completed her mission and even went on a shopping spree in Paris before returning to England with both the information and her new clothes, including a dress she had bought for Tania. Once back, she immediately volunteered for a second mission.

This new mission saw her and three colleagues parachuted into Limoges on 8 June 1944 to set up a new SOE network that would work to gather information about the enemy and relay it to SOE HQ back in London. Two days into the mission, she was travelling by car with a Resistance leader known as 'Anastase' when they ran into a German roadblock. During the attempted retreat she engaged the enemy in a fierce firefight until she ran out of ammunition. She was captured but her actions allowed Anastase to escape. Violette was taken to Limoges Prison before being moved to Fresnes Prison in Paris where she was tortured and interrogated by the SS.

In August, Violette and fellow SOE agents Denise Bloch and Lilian Rolfe were deported to Saarsbrücken transit camp before being transferred to Ravensbrück concentration camp and then on to a smaller camp at Torgau. At Torgau Violette came close to mounting an escape but her plans were discovered at the last minute. In October 1944 the women were moved again and put to work building a new runway just outside Königsberg. The conditions were brutal and the hard labour combined with a harsh winter took a toll on their physical wellbeing.

In January 1945 the three were sent back to Ravensbrück, unaware that their fate was already sealed. With defeat a matter of months away, the Nazis had taken the decision to eradicate all SOE agents before they could be liberated. In either late January or early February 1945, the women were led out to the camp's crematorium yard and shot in the back of the neck.

In December 1946, it was announced that Violette Szabo was to be awarded the George Cross and the following month four-year-old Tania, wearing the dress that her mother had purchased in Paris on her first mission, attended a private investiture by George VI at Buckingham Palace.

Films and Books

Such is Violette's fame that she has been the subject of three biographies: *Carve Her Name With Pride,* by R.J. Minney (1956), *Violette Szabo – The Life That I Have,* by Susan Ottaway (2002), and *Young, Brave and Beautiful,* by Tania Szabo (2007). In 1958, a film, also called *Carve Her Name With Pride,* starring Virginia McKenna, was released

45 Lieutenant Jimmie W. Monteith MoH

Jimmie W. Monteith was born on 1 July 1917 in Low Moor, Virginia. He attended Thomas Jefferson High School, graduating in 1937 before studying mechanical engineering at VPI (now Virginia Tech).

Monteith was drafted into the army in October 1941 and by March 1942 had been promoted to 2nd Lieutenant.

In April 1943, he was transferred to the 1st US Infantry Division, seeing action in North Africa and the invasion of Sicily, during which time he was promoted to 1st Lieutenant. He then found himself transferred to England to prepare for the upcoming invasion of Europe. For the Normandy invasion Monteith was a platoon commander for L Company, 16th Infantry Division, 1st US Infantry Division – known as 'Big Red One'.

Lieutenant Monteith and his men were part of the first attack wave on Omaha Beach. A War Department news release, quoting Sergeant Aaron B. Jones, a squad leader in Monteith's platoon, described what he did that day:

When we hit the beach, the air was thick with machine-gun, rifle, and shell fire. Lt. Monteith brought his men together and faced the first obstacle, layers of heavy barbed wire. After selecting a place where it could be blown open, he led men with a Bangalore torpedo in blasting the wire open.

Beyond this were two mine fields and he led the way through these. The field was traversed by machine-gun fire from the two enemy emplacements and from a pillbox, and when the men took cover, he stood studying the situation and then ran back to the beach.

On the beach were two tanks, buttoned up and blind because of heavy machine-gun fire that was directed on them. He walked through all that fire to bang on the sides of the

tanks and instruct the men inside to follow him. Then, walking in front he led the tanks to the pillbox, where they put it out of action. He then led his men against two machine-gun positions and knocked them out and then set up a defensive position to hold until more units could be brought from the beach. In that sector the enemy was not fighting from fixed positions but was moving around in the hedgerows and setting up automatic weapons. In this manner a fairly large group started an attack on the position and set up machine-guns on the flanks and rear. The Germans yelled to us to surrender because we were surrounded. Lt. Monteith did not answer but moved toward the sound of voices and launched a rifle grenade at them from 20 yards, knocking out the machine-gun position.

Even with a larger force the Germans couldn't break through our positions, so they set up two machine-guns and started spraying the hedgerow. Lt. Monteith got a squad of riflemen to open up on the machine-gun on the right flank. Under cover of the fire he sneaked up on the gun and threw hand grenades, which knocked out the position.

He then came back and crossed a 200-yard stretch of open field under fire to launch rifle grenades at the other machine-gun position. He either killed the crew or forced them to abandon the weapon. Back on the other flank enemy riflemen opened up on us

again, and Lt. Monteith started across the open field to help us fight them off but was killed by the fire of a light machine-gun that had been brought to our rear.

Monteith's heroism attracted the attention of the Supreme Commander of the Allied Forces himself. 'I must say that the thing looks like a Medal of Honor to me. This man was good.' Eisenhower wrote to his chief of staff about Monteith after the invasion, and in the process upgraded his award to the Medal of Honor from the Distinguished Service Cross he for which he was originally recommended.

Mrs Monteith received her son's Medal of Honor from Brigadier General Rupert E. Starr during a simple ceremony in her home in Richmond on 19 March 1945, and placed the medal around a photo of Jimmie that she kept on her mantelpiece. Monteith was buried in the temporary American St Laurent Cemetery, now the Normandy American Cemetery and Memorial, overlooking Omaha Beach.

46 Private Carlton W. Barrett MoH

Carlton William Barrett was born on 24 November 1919 in Fulton, New York and signed up to serve in the US Army on 29 October 1940, a month before his twenty-first birthday. At just 5ft 4in, Private Barrett was not only one of the smallest men to hit the beaches on D-Day, he was in one of the smallest units — a three-man reconnaissance team assigned to determine where the men of the 18th Infantry Regiment should gather after they waded ashore. The team would select the assembly areas, radio back to the command ship and await the regiment's arrival.

The beach in question carried the codename Omaha.

The 18th Regiment was a reserve regiment on D-Day and scheduled to land late in the morning. When Barrett eventually got to the beach, he found himself surrounded by dead and dying men. The pre-invasion bombardment had caused little damage to the enemy strongpoints and machine-gun posts that were overlooking the beach.. Most of the tanks and armour had not made it ashore, and many of the soldiers had been dropped off in the wrong sector - the entire beach was in chaos.

Instead of working out the assembly point, Barrett suddenly had a new mission — he had to save his comrades from being massacred in the surf. He immediately set to tending the wounded

men lying on the beach or entangled in the offshore barriers and stakes. Up to his neck in wind-whipped waves, he pulled or carried wounded men across a sandbar to an empty landing craft serving as medical evacuation vessel. He returned to the sea time and time again to rescue men who could not make it beyond the high-tide line, saving many lives in the process. All the while he was under constant enemy machine-gun fire. Meanwhile, US officers and NCOs were desperately working to save the landings and secure the beachhead. Barrett volunteered to act as messenger, carrying important messages and dispatches up and down the fire-swept beach.

The motto of the 18th Infantry Regiment is In Omina Paratus (Prepared For All Things) and Carlton Barrett certainly showed he was prepared for all things when his comrades needed him most. He transformed into an immensely strong leader in an intensely stressful situation, and in recognition of his actions on Omaha Beach, Private Barrett was awarded the Congressional Medal of Honor.

Barrett survived the war and remained in the army until retiring in June 1963 as a Staff Sergeant. He died in 1986, his Medal of Honor being donated to the First Division Museum at Cantigny.

Private Carlton W. Barrett with his Medal of Honor.

Medal of Honor citation:

For gallantry and intrepidity at the risk of his life above and beyond the call of duty on 6 June 1944, in the vicinity of St. Laurent-sur-Mer, France. On the morning of D-Day Pvt. Barrett, landing in the face of extremely heavy enemy fire, was forced to wade ashore through neck-deep water. Disregarding the personal danger, he returned to the surf again and again to assist his floundering comrades and save them from drowning. Refusing to remain pinned down by the intense barrage of small-arms and mortar fire poured at the landing points, Pvt. Barrett, working with fierce determination, saved many lives by carrying casualties to an evacuation boat lying offshore. In addition to his assigned mission as guide, he carried dispatches the length of the fire-swept beach; he assisted the wounded; he calmed the shocked; he arose as a leader in the stress of the occasion. His coolness and his dauntless daring courage while constantly risking his life during a period of many hours had an inestimable effect on his comrades and is in keeping with the highest traditions of the US Army.

47 Technician John J. Pinder (Jr) MoH

John Joseph Pinder Jr was born on 6 June 1912 in McKees Rocks, Pennsylvania. The oldest of three children, he had a sister, Martha and a brother, Harold. Harold would also see action in World War 2 in the US Airforce.

Pinder Jr joined the army as a radio technician just two days before his brother joined the US Air Force. He fitted in well to army life and it was not long before he was moving through the ranks, eventually working his way up to Level 5 Technician status while serving for 16th Infantry Regiment, 1st Infantry Division (known as the 'Big Red One') across North Africa and Sicily, before being moved to England for training in preparation for the Allied invasion of Western Europe.

On the morning of 6 June, 1944 Pinder found himself in a landing craft heading directly for Omaha Beach. As they approached the shore, they came under withering machine-gun and artillery fire, with many on Pinder's boat killed even before the disembarkation ramp had been lowered. Pinder jumped out into waist-deep sea water and struggled towards the beach, carrying around 300 lbs of radio equipment. He had only managed to travel a matter of yards before he was hit, suffering a major injury to the left side of his face as well as multiple shrapnel wounds across his body. Ignoring his wounds, Pinder carried on and carried his radio to shore. Refusing medical help, he returned to the water to retrieve radio equipment that had been abandoned and left floating in the sea. The water's edge was perhaps the most dangerous places for an Allied soldier to be at that time and he was under constant enemy fire. Pinder returned to the surf to collect equipment not once, but on three separate occasions.

On his third trip, he was hit in the leg by machine-gun fire. He valiantly crawled to shore with the last load of salvaged equipment. By this time, he was losing a lot of blood and growing weaker, but despite his deteriorating condition he refused help and stayed on the beach to get the radio equipment up and running, successfully establishing radio communications. It was while he was helping with this task that he was hit once more, this time fatally. For his heroic actions on Omaha Beach that morning, Pinder was posthumously awarded the Congressional Medal of Honor. John Joseph Pinder Jr was originally buried in the US Military Cemetery at St Laurent, France but his family requested their son's body be returned to the United States for re-burial. John J. Pinder Jr now rests in Grandview Cemetery, Florence, Pennsylvania.

John J. Pinder (right) pictured with his brother Harold H. Pinder while on leave in Bournemouth, England in January 1944.

Soldiers from the US 1st Division, 'Big Red One' embarking for Normandy, June 1944.

Medal of Honor citation:

For conspicuous gallantry and intrepidity above and beyond the call of duty on 6 June 1944, while serving with 16th Infantry Regiment, 1st Infantry Division, in action near Colleville-sur-Mer, France. On D-Day, Technician Fifth Grade Pinder landed on the coast 100 yards off shore under devastating enemy machine-gun and artillery fire which caused severe casualties among the boatload. Carrying a vitally important radio, he struggled towards shore in waist-deep water. Only a few yards from his craft he was hit by enemy fire and was gravely wounded. Technician 5th Grade Pinder never stopped. He made shore and delivered the radio. Refusing to take cover afforded, or to accept medical attention for his wounds, Technician 5th Grade Pinder, though terribly weakened by loss of blood and in fierce pain, on three occasions went into the fire-swept surf to salvage communication equipment. He recovered many vital parts and equipment, including another workable radio. On the third trip he was again hit, suffering machinegun bullet wounds in the legs. Still this valiant soldier would not stop for rest or medical attention. Remaining exposed to heavy enemy fire, growing steadily weaker, he aided in establishing the vital radio communication on the beach. While so engaged this dauntless soldier was hit for the third time and killed. The indomitable courage and personal bravery of Technician 5th Grade Pinder was a magnificent inspiration to the men with whom he served.

48 Lieutenant Colonel Leon R. Vance MoH

Leon Robert Vance Jr was born on 11 August 1916 and raised in Enid, Oklahoma, attending the local Enid schools from first grade all the way through to high school before attending the University of Oklahoma and then enrolling in the United States Military Academy at West Point on 1 July 1935. He graduated on 12 June 1939 and was commissioned as a Second Lieutenant in the US Infantry. He then went on to enrol in pilot training, earning his wings on 21 July 1940. After a number of local postings, he was eventually assigned to the 489th Bomb Group, based out of RAF Halesworth in England.

On 5 June 1944 Vance lead the 489th Bomb Group on a diversionary attack against German coastal defences over the Pas-de-Calais area of France. He was at the head of the formation, acting as lead navigator.

After an 09:00 take-off, Vance led his group up to their assigned 22,500 ft (6,900 m) altitude for the short flight to the French coast. The group approached the target area from the south in good order, but for some reason the bombs in Vance's aircraft failed to release and as a result none of the group released their bombs. Lieutenant Colonel Vance decided to turn around and carry out a second bomb run but as the formation approached the target a second time, it came under intense anti-aircraft fire.

Vance's lead B-24 immediately sustained heavy damage but continued its bomb run, this time successfully dropping all but one of its payload. By this time four crewmen were wounded, three of the four engines were disabled and the fuel lines had been ruptured. Shrapnel from the anti-aircraft fire had killed the pilot and wounded Vance, nearly severing his right foot, which became wedged under the co-pilot's seat. In the chaos that followed, comments on the interphone led Vance to believe that the crew's radio operator, wounded in the legs, was too seriously injured to be evacuated.

The failing B-24 lost altitude rapidly until the wounded co-pilot eventually regained control and prevented a stall by putting it into a steep glide to maintain airspeed. Despite shock from his own wound, Vance was able to assist the co-pilot while another member of the crew helped release his foot from under the seat and apply a makeshift tourniquet.

With all engines out and fuel leaking everywhere, the B-24 was too damaged to land safely and Vance ordered the crew to bail out. After most had complied, he took the controls and turned the aircraft back over the Channel, where the remainder parachuted into the sea. He decided to attempt a water landing in the belief that the injured radio operator was still on the aircraft, even though B-24s were notoriously ill-suited for 'ditching'.

Although the bomber managed to survive the impact largely intact, its dorsal gun turret collapsed and pinned Vance inside the flooded cockpit as the bomber sank. Fortunately, an explosion blew him clear of the wreckage and he was eventually able to inflate his Mae West. After searching for the radio operator, Vance swam towards shore. He was finally picked up by an RAF Air-Sea Rescue launch after fifty minutes.

For his astonishing bravery, staying with his plane and trying to save all of the crew, Lieutenant Colonel Vance was awarded the Congressional Medal of Honor.

After several weeks of recuperation in England, Vance was sent back to the United States with a group of seventeen other US casualties from the Normandy campaign. Once he was back home in the US, the plan was for him to receive further treatment, including a possible prosthetic foot. Unfortunately, the C-54 Skymaster transport plane used for the journey back to the US crashed at sea on 26 July. Despite an air-sea rescue attempt, all occupants perished.

The recommendation for the Congressional Medal of Honor was confirmed in orders on 4 January 1945, but his widow requested that the awards ceremony be delayed until the medal could be presented to their daughter. On 11 October 1946, Major General James P. Hodges, Commander of the 2nd Bomb Division when Vance was assigned to it, made the presentation to Sharon Vance, aged just three, at Enid Army Air Base.

US Air Force Photo

B-24 Liberator similar to what Vance would have flown in.

This was the only CMoH to be awarded to any B-24 crewman in the US 8th Air Force

49 Brigadier General Theodore Roosevelt III MoH

Theodore (Ted) Roosevelt III was born in Long Island, New York on 1 September 1887 and was the eldest son of President Theodore Roosevelt and First Lady Edith Roosevelt. After attending the Groton School in Massachusetts, Ted attended Harvard where he gained membership to the prestigious Porcellian Club. After graduating from Harvard in 1909, Ted became a partner in the Philadelphia investment banking firm of Montgomery, Clothier and Tyler, although he longed to serve in the US military.

America joining World War 1 gave Roosevelt the opportunity to realise his military ambition and he quickly volunteered to go to France. His wife, Eleanor, also went to Europe with him, taking up a role with YMCA female volunteers behind the front lines. Roosevelt quickly established a name for himself as an excellent leader of men, repeatedly leading them personally into battle. He cared for the men under his command a great deal – one time even purchasing his entire battalion new boots out of his own money. He eventually took command of the 26th Regiment in the US 1st Division but still led right from the front, leading to him being gassed and wounded at Soissons in the summer of 1918.

For his actions during World War 1, Roosevelt received the American Distinguished Service Cross, the French Croix de Guerre (1914–18) and the French Chevalier Légion d'honneur.

After the war Roosevelt served as an officer with the Army Reserves and from 1919 he held a number of public positions, including serving as the Governor of Puerto Rico and Governor General of the Philippines. After leaving public service in 1933, he accepted a position as Vice President with publishing company Doubleday Doran.

By 1940, the threat of war for America was looming large and Roosevelt attended a military refresher course and was promoted to the rank of Colonel. He returned to active duty in April 1941 and was given command of the 26th Infantry Regiment, part of the 1st Infantry Division, the same unit he fought with in World War 1. Late in 1941, he was promoted to the one-star general officer rank of Brigadier General.

From 1942, with America firmly in the war, he travelled with his regiment to North Africa. As in the previous war, he became known as a general who was never far from the front line. He was one of those leaders who preferred the heat of the battle to the relative comfort of a HQ position way behind the lines. He led his men in an attack on Oran, Algeria on 8 November 1942 as part of Operation Torch and was also right in thick of it during the Allied invasion of Sicily.

In February 1944, Roosevelt was transferred to England to help prepare for Operation Neptune with the US 4th Infantry Division. He desperately wanted to lead his men on to the beaches, but several verbal requests to do so were rejected by the division's Commanding General, Major General Raymond 'Tubby' Barton. Not to be denied, Roosevelt sent in a written request;

The force and skill with which the first elements hit the beach and proceed may determine the ultimate success of the operation.... With troops engaged for the first time, the behavior pattern of all is apt to be set by those first engagements. [It is] considered that accurate information of the existing situation should be available for each succeeding element as it lands. You should have when you get to shore an overall picture in which you can place confidence. I believe I can contribute materially on all of the above by going in with the assault companies. Furthermore, I personally know both officers and men of these advance units and believe that it will steady them to know that I am with them.

Barton grudgingly approved this written request, and as a result Roosevelt was the only general on D-Day to go ashore

Memorial and Museum of Bloody Gulch

Brigadier General Theodore Roosevelt III pictured just hours before he collapsed of a heart attack. Sainte-Mère-Églilse, 12 July 1944.

as part of the first wave of troops, and at the age of fifty-six, was the oldest Allied man in the entire invasion. He was also the only person who had a son take part in the operation; Captain Quentin Roosevelt II was among the first wave of soldiers at Omaha Beach.

Not only was Brigadier General Roosevelt in the first wave of men assigned to hit Utah Beach, when the ramp went down on his landing craft, he was one of the first soldiers to disembark – leading from the front as he always did. With his walking stick (needed due to arthritis, as a result from old wounds from World War 1) and carrying a pistol, he personally made a reconnaissance of the area immediately to the rear of the beach to locate the causeways that were to be used for the advance inland. The first tranche of landing craft had drifted south in strong winds, resulting in the men being a mile away from the designated landing zones. He returned to the point of landing and contacted the commanders of the two battalions, Lieutenant Colonels Conrad C. Simmons and Carlton O. MacNeely, and co-ordinated the attack on the enemy positions. Opting to fight from where they had landed rather than trying to move to their assigned positions, Roosevelt declared, 'We'll start the war from right here!'

The impromptu plan worked. With the enemy hitting the beach with artillery and small arms fire, each wave of infantry was welcomed on to the beach by Roosevelt, who then calmly and clearly informed them of their new positions and objectives. He inspired the men with humour and confidence, reciting poetry and telling stories in an effort to calm them. Despite being almost continually under fire, he worked as a self-appointed beach master, organising vehicles, tanks and equipment so they could all get inland and off the beach as quickly as possible. One GI later reported that seeing the Roosevelt walking around, apparently unaffected by the enemy fire, even when clods of earth fell down on

him, gave him the courage to get on with the job, saying if the general is like that it cannot be that bad.

He was later cited for exemplary courage and behaviour, and was awarded the Medal of Honor for his actions.

As well as the arthritis, Roosevelt also suffered with heart trouble, which he kept secret from army doctors and his superiors. On 12 July 1944 Roosevelt died of a heart attack in Méautis, some 15 miles from Sainte-Mère-Église. He had spent part of the day in a long conversation with his son, Captain Quentin Roosevelt II, but at around 22:00 he collapsed and died around midnight, despite the best efforts of the medics who attended him. On the day of his death, he had been selected by Lieutenant General Omar Bradley, Commander of the US First Army, for promotion to the rank of two-star major general and the command of the 90th Infantry Division. These recommendations were sent to Eisenhower for approval. When Eisenhower called the next morning to approve them, he was told that Roosevelt had died during the night.

Roosevelt was initially buried at Sainte-Mère-Église, but was eventually moved to the Normandy American Cemetery. In 1955, his younger brother, 2nd Lieutenant Quentin Roosevelt, who had been killed during World War 1, was also moved to the Normandy cemetery and re-interred next to his brother. He is the only World War 1 casualty in the whole cemetery.

The final resting place of Theodore Roosevelt, Jr. in Normandy.

Awards

Medal of Honor (posthumously), Distinguished Service Cross, Distinguished Service Medal, Silver Star with three oak clusters, Legion of Merit, Purple Heart, Victory Medal, American Defense Service Medal, American Campaign Medal, European-African-Middle Eastern Campaign Medal, World War II Victory Medal (posthumously), French Légion d'honneur, French Croix de Guerre 1914–18, Medal of Liberated France

....

When his father's medal was belatedly awarded in 2001 for heroism in the Spanish-American War, the two men became one of only two father/sons to receive the award. (The other pairing was Civil War Army 1 Lieutenant Arthur MacArthur Jr and his son, World War 2 General Douglas MacArthur)

Medal of Honor citation:

For gallantry and intrepidity at the risk of his life above and beyond the call of duty on 6 June 1944, while serving as a commander in the 4th Infantry Division in France. After two verbal requests to accompany the leading assault elements in the Normandy invasion had been denied, Brigadier General Roosevelt's written request for this mission was approved and he landed with the first wave of the forces assaulting the enemy-held beaches. He repeatedly led groups from the beach, over the seawall and established them inland. His valor, courage, and presence in the very front of the attack and his complete unconcern at being under heavy fire inspired the troops to heights of enthusiasm and self-sacrifice. Although the enemy had the beach under constant direct fire, Brigadier General Roosevelt moved from one locality to another, rallying men around him, directed and personally led them against the enemy. Under his seasoned, precise, calm, and unfaltering leadership, assault troops reduced beach strong points and rapidly moved inland with minimum casualties. He thus contributed substantially to the successful establishment of the beachhead in France.

50 Lieutenant Walter D. Ehlers MoH

Walter David Ehlers was born on 7 May 1921, in Junction City, Kansas. He and his older brother Roland joined the army together in November 1940 and fought side by side in North Africa and Sicily.

In the spring of 1944, they were both stationed in England, busy training for the long-awaited Allied invasion of northern France. The brothers were both assigned to K Company of the 18th Regiment, 1st Infantry Division, and were destined to both be part of the second assault wave on Omaha Beach. However, the officers of the division, anticipating heavy D-Day casualties and wanting to ensure that at least one of the brothers survived the invasion, took the decision to split them up.

Walter Ehlers led his twelve-man reconnaissance team on to the beach through head-high water and eventually made it off the beach through German minefields without a single casualty. The next day Walter learned that his brother Roland was missing in action.

On 9 June, Sergeant Ehlers single-handedly killed four German soldiers while on patrol amid the Normandy hedgerows, then destroyed three machine-gun nests and a mortar position, at one point leading a bayonet charge. The following day, after penetrating deep into enemy territory, his team found themselves under intense fire and were forced to withdraw. By standing up and attracting enemy fire on to himself, he enabled his men to withdraw to safety. He was shot in the back but refused to be evacuated. Instead he carried a wounded member of his team to safety before returning to the field of fire to pick up his rifle. For these heroic actions, Sergeant Ehlers would be awarded the Congressional Medal of Honor. A few days later he learned that his brother Roland had been killed on D-Day just as he was getting out of his landing craft.

Sergeant Ehlers was invested with the Medal of Honor on 11 December 1944 and subsequently promoted to Lieutenant.

He died on 20 February 2014, aged ninety-two. He was the last surviving Medal of Honor winner from the Normandy campaign.

Medal of Honor citation:

For conspicuous gallantry and intrepidity at the risk of his life above and beyond the call of duty on 9-10 June 1944, near Goville, France. S/Sgt. Ehlers, always acting as the spearhead of the attack, repeatedly led his men against heavily defended enemy strong points exposing himself to deadly hostile fire whenever the situation required heroic and courageous leadership. Without waiting for an order, S/Sgt. Ehlers, far ahead of his men, led his squad against a strongly defended enemy strong point, personally killing 4 of an enemy patrol who attacked him en route. Then crawling forward under withering machinegun fire, he pounced upon the guncrew and put it out of action. Turning his attention to 2 mortars protected by the crossfire of 2 machineguns, S/Sgt. Ehlers led his men through this hail of bullets to kill or put to flight the enemy of the mortar section, killing 3 men himself. After mopping up the mortar positions, he again advanced on a machinegun, his progress effectively covered by his squad. When he was almost on top of the gun he leaped to his feet and, although greatly outnumbered, he knocked out the position single-handed. The next day, having advanced deep into enemy territory, the platoon of which S/Sgt. Ehlers was a member, finding itself in an untenable position as the enemy brought increased mortar, machinegun, and small arms fire to bear on it, was ordered to withdraw. S/Sgt. Ehlers, after his squad had covered the withdrawal of the remainder of the platoon, stood up and by continuous fire at the semicircle of enemy placements, diverted the bulk of the heavy hostile fire on himself, thus permitting the members of his own squad to withdraw. At this point, though wounded himself, he carried his wounded automatic rifleman to safety and then returned fearlessly over the shell-swept field to retrieve the automatic rifle which he was unable to carry previously. After having his wound treated, he refused to be evacuated, and returned to lead his squad. The intrepid leadership, indomitable courage, and fearless aggressiveness displayed by S/Sgt. Ehlers in the face of overwhelming enemy forces serve as an inspiration to others.

51 SS-Hauptsturmführer Michael Wittmann KC

Michael Wittmann was born on 22 April 1914 in the small village of Vogelthal in the Oberpfalz region of Bavaria., The young Wittmann joined his father and younger brother in running the family farm. It was hard, manual work, but it was here where Wittmann developed many of the basic skills such as team work and mechanical know-how, that were to serve him so well later in life.

In 1934 he joined the Reichsarbeitsdienst, or Reich Labour Service, a well-organised paramilitary organisation. It was during this time that he first encountered a panzer – the Panzerkampfwagen I – and he was immediately drawn to it. By 1937 he was accepted into the elite Leibstandarte SS Adolf Hitler as an armoured car crewman and went on to gain a reputation for himself. In the spring of 1944, after achieving celebratory status on the Eastern Front, he was given command of 2nd Company, 101st SS Heavy Panzer Battalion. He and his gunner, Bobby Woll, had by then been credited with destroying an astonishing 119 enemy armoured fighting vehicles.

The Normandy invasion prompted Wittmann's battalion to be moved, his company arriving on the scene during the evening of 12 June, by which time Allied formations had reached the outskirts of Caen. On the morning of 13 June, Wittmann offered to use his Tiger to carry out a reconnaissance of the surrounding area of Villers-Bocage. Unknown to him, the British had set out earlier in the morning and were already on their way to the town with the intention of taking the nearby Hill 213 and securing the road to Caen.

While at his command post located some 150 metres from Hill 213, Wittmann saw a large convoy of Allied vehicles belonging to the 4th County of London Yeomanry and 1st Rifle Brigade, part of the 22nd Armoured Brigade of the 7th Armoured Division – the renowned 'Desert Rats' – heading towards Hill 213.

This rather enticing opportunity provided Wittmann with an opportunity too good to pass up. Without alerting HQ, and with precious little German armour in the vicinity to act as back up, he decided to strike.

While Wittman moved into position towards the rear of the column, a few other Tigers from his group moved out towards Hill 213 in an effort to cut the enemy off, who had conveniently stopped by the roadside for a cup of tea. Wittmann approached slowly in this Tiger, then charged towards the rear of the column, the British crews had no time to react or return to their vehicles, let alone organise some sort of defensive position against the mighty

Tiger. Instead, they fled. In a matter of minutes Wittmann destroyed fourteen vehicles and two anti-tank guns before heading down the road towards the town, destroying three more M3 Stuart tanks, the scout car belonging to the RHQ Intelligence Officer and the half-track truck belonging to the regimental Medical Officer in the process.

Despite a close shave with a Sherman Firefly, Wittmann advanced through the town of Villers-Bocage with relative ease. It was too risky to continue his advance alone, so Wittmann decided to head back to his own lines. However, his tank was hit on its tracks – its weakest point – by anti-tank fire and quickly became immobile. Wittmann and his crew had no choice but to bail from the stricken Tiger and escape on foot, some 7 kilometres, back to his HQ.

Already a national hero, he was awarded the swords to the Knight's Cross for his daring actions, destroying a total of approximately twenty-five enemy vehicles. His citation ended, 'With the count of 13th June, Wittmann has achieved a total number of victories of 138 enemy tanks and 132 anti-tank guns with his personal Panzer.'

SS-Hauptsturmführer Michael Wittmann was killed in action on 8 August 1944, when his Tiger tank was destroyed during an ambush near the French town of Saint-Aignan-de-Cramesnil. Wittmann and his crew were buried in an unmarked grave at the site of his death. In 1983, the German war graves commission located the burial site and re-interred Wittmann and his crew at the La Cambe German war cemetery.

'They never left the road. They were so surprised that they took flight, but not with their vehicles, instead they jumped out, and I shot up the battalion's vehicles as I drove by'

SS-Hauptsturmführer
Michael Wittmann KC.

Landing Craft, Vehicle & Personnel (LCVP)

The Landing Craft, Vehicle and Personnel (LCVP) was arguably the most important American landing craft of World War 2 and used extensively in amphibious landings across the globe. More commonly known as 'Higgins Boats' after their designer, Andrew Higgins, these flat-bottomed landing craft delivered tens of thousands of American and Allied troops on to the beaches of Europe, North Africa and the Pacific.

The genesis of the LCVP can be traced back to the wetlands of South Louisiana during the 1930s, when Higgins Industries developed a workboat known as 'Eureka',

which was designed specifically for use in the swamps and marshes of the area. Its unique design meant the boat was quick, agile, could operate in just 18 inches of water and run through vegetation and over debris without damaging its propeller. More importantly, it could also run right up tight to the shoreline and extract itself without damage.

The US Marine Corps expressed an interest in the Eureka boat and in 1938 carried out a series of tests, in which Higgins' boat surpassed the performance of similar craft developed by the US Navy. The only downside was that men

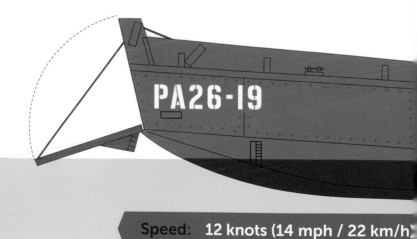

Speed: 12 knots (14 mph / 22 km/h)

Length:

and equipment had to be disembarked from the boat over the sides – making escaping the boat slow and dangerous. The Japanese had been using ramps to disembark troops since 1937 and when the Marine Corps suggested it as a possible modification, Higgins got on with the re-design straight away, building three full-sized craft for testing.

On 26 May 1941, senior officials from the US Navy and the US Marine Corps attended testing. One off-loaded a truck, and another one loaded and unloaded thirty-six Higgins employees – simulating troops. The trials were a success and very soon afterwards the US government started placing large orders. Higgins industries had to work around the clock

Troops: | **Crew:**
36 | **4**

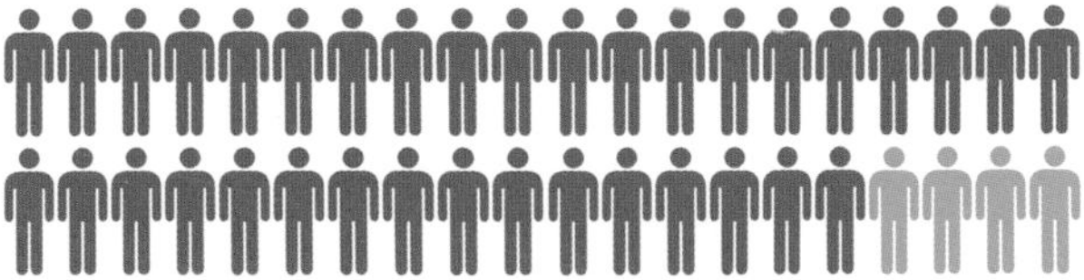

Capacity –
6,000 lb / (2,700 kg)
vehicles, or 8,100 lb
(3,700 kg) general cargo

Armament –
2 x .30 cal (7.62 mm)
Browning machine-guns

to meet demand – peak production was over 700 craft per month, but very soon a network of subcontractors was established to raise production even more. In the end, over 20,000 landing craft were produced.

Powered by a 225-horsepower diesel engine producing a top speed of 12 knots, it would sway in choppy seas, causing seasickness. Since its sides and rear were made of plywood, it offered limited protection from enemy fire but also reduced cost and saved steel. The steel ramp at the front could be lowered quickly, making it possible for the Higgins boat to swiftly disembark men and supplies, reverse itself off the beach, and head back out to the supply ship for another load within three to four minutes.

In 1964, the then US President Eisenhower suggested Andrew Higgins was 'the man who won the war for us', explaining that 'If Higgins had not designed and built those LCVPs, we never could have landed over an open beach. The whole strategy of the war would have been different.'

An LCVP from USS *Thomas Jefferson* (APA-30) pulls away from the shore with a full load of troops who will be carried to invasion shipping in the harbour. Photographed at a southern English port during pre-invasion loading operations.

US National Archives

More than
23,000
LCVPs were built between 1942 and 1945

Higgins Industries – An Equal Opportunity employer

The Higgins factory in New Orleans was the first in the city with a racially integrated workforce. All 30,000 members of staff were paid equal wages according to their job rating

'If Higgins had not designed and built those LCVPs, we never could have landed over an open beach. The whole strategy of war would have been different.'

General Dwight D. Eisenhower

53 Landing Ship, Tank

The Dunkirk evacuations in 1940 demonstrated to the Admiralty the need for large, ocean-going ships capable of decent carrying capacity and shore-to-shore delivery enabling tanks and other vehicles to be either deposited on or picked up from beaches. In 1940, early plans for an invasion of Western Europe were already being drawn up, and this included the need to get hundreds of thousands of men ashore right under the nose of the enemy, along with the requisite kit, guns, ammunition and supplies to allow the troops to first build a significant beachhead before pushing inland.

In 1941, an Admiralty consortium met with the US Navy's Bureau of Ships regarding the development and manufacture of such vessels and within a few days the first design sketches were drawn up and sent to London, where they were approved immediately.

These sketches would prove to be the basic design template for the LST (Landing Ship, Tank), a vessel that would eventually prove to be one of, if not the most important of all landing craft used on D-Day.

Originally the requirements for the LST was a ship that was 280 feet long, however this was stretched out to 328 feet to allow for improved weight distribution that made it ride higher in the water when approaching beaches.

By January 1942 the first scale model had been built and was being tested in Washington, D.C. and just six months later the keel of the first LST was laid down at Newport News, Virginia. Such was the priority given to the construction of the LSTs that an aircraft carrier in the process of being constructed was taken out of dock to make way for them.

By 1943 the construction time for an LST was four months. By the end of the war this was down to just two months. Although every effort was made to keep manufacturer and design as standard as possible to help with production time, there were some minor modifications over time. Some of the most significant upgrades included inserting a ramp instead of an elevator between the main deck and tank deck, improvements in armament and the addition of a distilling plant to ensure a constant supply of drinking water.

US National Archives

USS LST-325 unloads on a Normandy beach at low tide, 12 June 1944.

The LST's flat bottom and twin bow doors permitted direct delivery of heavy vehicles to the invasion beach. Trucks, tanks and other vehicles were carried in the so-called tank deck, while smaller landing craft could be carried on the top deck. Apart from delivering vital troops and equipment to the invasion beaches, LSTs were also used as frontline hospital ships, evacuating thousands of casualties directly to England and safety. Over 200 LSTs were used in the D-Day landings, at the time this represented almost two-thirds of all LSTs available to Allied fleet units worldwide. Despite being given the moniker 'Large Slow Target' by the many troops it transported and its own crew, only five craft were lost during the invasion.

> 'Let there be built great ships which can cast up on a beach in any weather large numbers of the heaviest tanks'

Sir Winston Churchill,
7 July 1940

An LST could carry up to

20

Sherman Tanks

US
72

Speed: 12 knots (14 mph / 22 km/h)

Length: 328 ft

Four LSTs take vehicles aboard during pre-invasion loading operations at an English port, c. early June 1944. Ships present include: USS LST-496; USS LST-506 and USS LST-291.

'It was pretty traumatic. On D-Day, arriving at the beach, the noise, the gunfire, the amount of ships, was something beyond your wildest dreams, you'd never seen anything like it'

Norman Pimblett – LST Crew

By 28 September 1944, LSTs had transported

41,035

wounded men back across the English Channel from the Normandy beaches

Numbers of LSTs made during World War 2 :

1,015

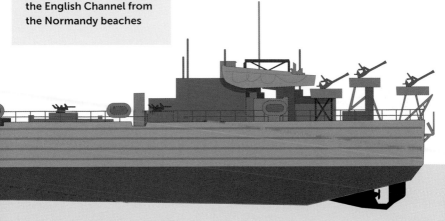

54 Landing Craft, Tank

The landing craft, tank was an amphibious assault craft for landing tanks onto beachheads. It was initially developed by the British Royal Navy and later by the United States Navy during World War 2.

The design of the ship was very simple. The crew's quarters were in the very stern of the ship and accessed via a ladder. There was no refrigeration and cooking was done on a simple stove, which also served as a heater. Next to the crew's mess was the engine room and above was the bridge, wheelhouse and officers' cabin. The rest of the ship was tank space. The entire ship's bottom was flat which allowed good access to the beaches for unloading but made them notoriously difficult to keep on course in strong winds or currents. The deck of the tank space was equipped with drainage holes, and large rings were in place for fastening the vehicles firmly to the deck so that they would stay in position during a rough passage at sea. Heavy steel chocks were used to fasten the vehicles to the anchoring rings.

The design was subtly enhanced over time and with each new release the LCT became slightly larger and slightly easier to handle. There were also a number of modified conversions made for specific purposes such as the Landing Craft, Tank (Armoured) which boasted armour plate over the engine room, fuel tanks and wheel house, along with the construction of tank ramp platforms on the tank deck to carry two Centaur tanks. It was intended that on D-Day these Centaurs would provide direct fire on to the beaches during the run-in to land and then support where needed from the water's edge. However, on Gold Beach only two out of the sixteen LCT(A) vessels arrived at the beach on time and took part in the fire plan. A mixture of overloading, bad weather and shoddy workmanship resulted in many of the LCT(A)s being unseaworthy and prone to flooding. A similar story played out on the other beaches.

Another conversion was the Landing Craft Tank (Rocket) or LCT(R). Designed for shore bombardment before the first assault wave attacked, these were some of the most important and deadly support craft in the whole invasion armada. Two types of LCT were converted – the Mk.II and the Mk.III – and they carried 792- and 1,064 5-inch rocket launchers respectively. The LCT(R) was capable of firing between 800 and 1000 rockets in salvos of either 24, 26, 39 or 42.

837 LCTs were involved in the D-Day landings, making it the most numerous vessel in the invasion.

Men rest on the ramp of USS LCT-528, stranded by low tide, 15 June 1944.

Capacity

5 30 ton tanks

Commandos of the 50th (Northumbrian) Infantry Division of the British Army coming ashore at Gold Beach on 6 June 1944. In the background are two Landing Craft Tanks.

Each rocket from the LCT(R) had a bursting radius of 30 yards and it was estimated that the shock power from one salvo of rockets was 2.5 times greater that that of a battleship salvo

Numbers of LCTs built: **470**

Displacement: 286 short tons (259 t) (landing)

Length: 117 ft 6 in (35.81 m)

Beam: 32 ft (9.8 m)

Speed: 8 knots (15 km/h; 9.2 mph)

Range: 700 nmi (1,300 km) at 7 kn (13 km/h)

'We had landing craft fitted with a hundred rockets and when these went off with a "Woosh! Woosh! Woosh! Woosh! Woosh! Woosh! Woosh!" they would all stream inland and there would be vast series of explosions on shore. You couldn't help thinking that there would be nothing left surviving underneath'

Engine Room Artificer Ronald Jesse, Royal Navy HMS *Belfast*

55 Landing Craft, Assault

Landing Craft Assault (LCA) were the basic landing craft of the British Army and used extensively throughout World War 2 to carry troops from larger transport ships to attack enemy held coastlines. Typically constructed of hardwood planking covered with armour plate, this shallow-draft, barge-like boat could carry up to thirty-five men to shore at a steady 7 knots (8mph / 13 km/h).

Throughout the war, LCAs were transported to various landing zones either by being towed by larger craft or under their own steam. For larger operations such as Operation Torch or Operation Overlord, the flotillas of LCAs were carried to the invasion areas by groups of Landing Ship Infantry (LSI) which sailed to a predefined 'Lowering Position' normally about 6 to 11 miles (10 to 17km) from shore. An LCA was swung down to the level of the loading deck and the men climbed aboard. When fully loaded, the LCA was lowered into the water and sent on its way.

For D-Day, hundreds of LCAs carried British and Commonwealth troops ashore at Juno, Gold, and Sword beaches. The final approaches to the invasion beaches were not without challenges: the invasion itself took place in daylight in full view of the enemy and differing high water times across the landing zones meant different approach times for different beaches. However, the weather was the main problem on D-Day, with the sea conditions off the Normandy coast resulting in large waves and strong currents, which were outside the normal operation scope of the LCA. Overlord, however, was not a normal operation, so the LCAs had to battle through. The shallow draft boats did not cope well with the rough waters and were tossed about with vigour. Only the hardiest of sea-legs were not affected by severe sea-sickness on the final approaches to the beaches. It was not a glamourous start to the greatest seaborne invasion in history.

Over on Omaha Beach, specially modified LCAs were carrying highly trained men for a very particular mission. Each one of the ten LCAs making up Flotillas 510 and 522 that carried the 2nd Ranger Battalion to Pointe du Hoc was fitted with three pairs of rocket tubes. These rocket tubes fired grapnels which launched rope ladders, toggle ropes and ¾ inch plain ropes towards the cliff face to enable the Rangers to start their ascent – all of which were stowed down the sides of each LCA. Other D-Day LCAs were modified to carry light weapons such as a Lewis or a Bren gun. In total around 2,000 units were built.

Displacement: 286 short tons (259 t) (landing)

Length: 41.5 ft (12.6 m)

Beam: 32 ft (9.8 m)

Speed: 10 knots (19 km/h; 12 mph) (light), 6 knots (11 km/h; 6.9 mph) (loaded)

Armament: one Bren light machine-gun or two Lewis machine-guns

Troops:
30-35

Crew:
4

British Commandos of the 50th (Northumbrian) Infantry Division coming ashore from Landing Craft Assault (LCA) at Gold Beach.

'To keep the LCA going and stop it from being swamped took your undivided attention, to steer the thing and keep it afloat. You weren't able to stand back and see what was going on around you for the majority of the time. It was only when we got in amongst the beach obstacles that it really hit home that we could be in for a lot trouble, because there was so much firepower going on'

Leading Seaman John Tarbit, LCA Coxswain

Numbers of LSAs built approximately

2,000

Lost –1939–45:
371
(267 in 1944)

56 DUKW

The DUKW was the result of a design partnership between Sparkman & Stephens and General Motors Corporation (GMC) in the USA in an effort to solve the problem of resupplying units which had just been put ashore during a military amphibious landing. Initial designs were rejected by the US military, but when an experimental DUKW rescued a stranded US Coast Guard patrol boat that had ran aground in stormy weather military opposition melted away.

The DUKW made its operational debut during the seaborne invasion of Sicily in 1943. The crafts worked extremely well and enabled men and equipment to be loaded directly on to the invasion beaches with relative ease. The key was the fact the DUKW could be driven directly from the water onto land – it was basically a GMC six-wheel military truck with a propeller and extra waterproofing. Before the DUKW, large ships had to sail up as close as they could to the shore for the slow and dangerous process of unloading, DUKWs made this whole process much easier, quicker and safer because they could be pre-loaded out at sea, then drive right out of the larger ship and directly onto land. It was nothing short of revolutionary.

Not surprisingly, after the success of the Sicily campaign, the DUKWs were used in large numbers during Operation Overlord, although off the coast of Normandy their success was decidedly mixed. At Omaha, DUKWs were loaded up to the max with food, medicine, ammunition and a heavy howitzer or cannon crammed into each boat. Under normal circumstances, this would not have been an issue – the DUKW was designed to carry heavy loads – but these were not normal circumstances. The sea was very rough and after rolling off of the mothership, the DUKWs carrying howitzers began to sink almost immediately. Only one of those ships managed to get ashore in one piece. As well as putting soldiers and equipment onshore during D-Day, many DUKWs were employed in evacuating wounded soldiers from the invasion beaches towards the end of D-Day and during the subsequent days after the invasion.

Over 21,000 DUKWs were manufacturered before production ended in 1945 and examples could be seen working well in all theatres of the war. The majority were supplied to the US Army and the US Marine Corps although around 2,000 were delivered to Britain as part of the Lend-Lease programme. After the war, entrepreneurs began using DUKW boats to give water tours for tourists – some can still be seen in service today.

Ducks

The name 'DUKW' corresponded to
General Motors' manufacturing code
D = 1942 model
U = amphibious / utility
K = all-wheel drive
W = dual rear axles.
Soldiers simplified this
by calling them 'duck'.

US National Archives

Army DUKW amphibious truck
brings supplies ashore.

Numbers built 1942-45

21,147

Speed: 50 mph (80 km/h) on road,
6.4 mph (6 kn; 10 km/h) in water

Weight: 13,600 lb
(6,200 kg) empty
Length: 31 ft (9.45 m)
Width: 8 ft (2.44 m)
Height: 8 ft 10 in (2.69 m)
with top up / 7 ft 1 in
(2.16 m) minimum

Crew:

1

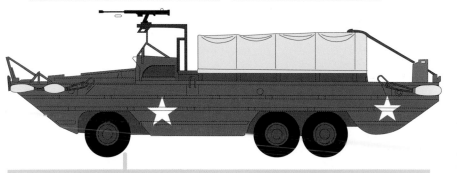

Tyre pressure versatility

The DUKW was the first vehicle to allow the driver to vary the tyre pressure
from inside the cab. The tyres could be fully inflated for hard surfaces, such as
roads, and less inflated for softer surfaces, especially beach sand. This added to
its versatility as an amphibious vehicle and is a feature that is now standard on
many military vehicles

57 *Leichter Ladungsträger* Goliath tanks

The *Leichter Ladungsträger* Goliath (Goliath Light Charge Carrier) was a name given to two German unmanned, single-use demolition vehicles, used widely across all theatres the Germans were involved in throughout World War 2. Specifically, the two models were the electrically powered Sd.Kfz. 302 and the petrol-engine powered Sd.Kfz. 303a and 303b. They were often known as Beetle Tanks among Allied forces.

When the Germans invaded France in 1941, they discovered the prototype of a French miniature tracked vehicle developed by engineer Adolphe Kégresse. This discovery gave German military engineers the idea of creating a small tracked vehicle that could be controlled remotely and deliver and detonate explosives. In 1942, the first electric Goliaths were introduced to some engineering and specialist panzer units and were used to destroy tanks, strongpoints, bridges and other structures. They had a cable of some 650 metres to enable remote operation and were able to carry 60 kg of explosives.

The Goliath was transported to the battlefield on a two-wheeled trailer. Once a target had been identified, the electric motor was started and the Goliath was directed on its course by remote control. This consisted of a control box linked to the vehicle by cable, which enabled the operator to steer the vehicle left or right and remotely detonate the on board charge.

A second version of the Goliath (SdKfz 303) was developed which was powered by a by a Zundapp 703cc, two-cylinder motorcycle engine. This upgraded version was bigger, heavier, more reliable and able to carry up to 100 kg of explosives. Both versions were designed as single-use vehicles and were destroyed by the detonation of their explosive cargo.

Goliaths were used on all fronts where the Wehrmacht fought from early 1942, including being used for mine clearance during the Battle of Kursk, at Anzio in Italy in April 1944 and against the Polish resistance during the Warsaw Uprising.

Despite being made in their thousands, they were not all together reliable, with operators reporting that the cables were prone to damage, they were too slow to catch a moving tank and often rolled over on uneven ground. They were vulnerable to small arms fire and would get stuck on steep hills. Many failed to get close to their targets, but if they did, the results were often spectacular.

Despite these operational glitches, Goliaths were widely deployed along the Atlantic Wall to protect the European coastline against an Allied invasion, including in and around the Normandy beaches. However, most Goliaths that were in position at Normandy were rendered useless due to artillery fire severing their cables.

Large numbers of Goliaths were captured by the Allies. Although they were examined with interest by Allied intelligence, they were deemed to have little military value. Nevertheless, the Goliath helped to lay the foundations for post-war advances in the field of remote-controlled military vehicle and drone technologies.

US National Archives

With a DUKW in the background, a member of the US Navy's 2nd Beach Battalion tinkers with a captured German Goliath tracked mine, or 'beetle' on Utah Beach on 11 June 1944.

Goliath Sd.kfz 302

Engine: Two Electric Motors – 2 x 2.5 hp (1.9 kW)

Armament: 60 kg (130 lb) explosive charge

Numbers built 1942-45

7,564

Goliath Sd.kfx 303a/b

Engine: Zündapp SZ7 / 2-cylinder – 12.5 hp (9.3 kW)

Armament: 100 kg (220 lb) explosive charge

Numbers built 1943-45

4,929

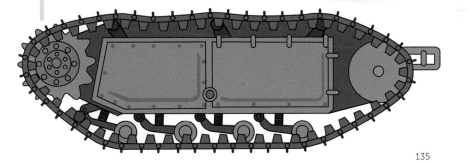

58 Fighter Direction Tenders

The section of the French coast selected for the invasion of Europe was over 80 miles from the English coastline and at the very outer limits of the English coastal radar network. The concept of operating ground radar equipment from specially converted sea vessels was proven during the invasion of Sicily in July 1943 and Air Chief Marshall Leigh-Mallory pushed hard for similar vessels to be used planning for Operation Neptune.

The plan for Normandy was to choose three Landing Ship Tank (LST) vessels and have them converted to become air surveillance and control ships. Officially designated as Fighter Direction Tenders (FDTs), each ship was refitted and equipped with the latest radar technology, including Type 15 and Type 11 radar, the latest IFF interrogators/responders, aircraft Interception beacons, VHF radio telephony and wireless telegraphy sets. Once converted, each vessel boasted a displacement of 3,700 tons and a length of about 328 feet – comparable to a Royal Navy destroyer. They carried a navy crew of eight officers and ninety-two ratings, and an air crew of 19 RAF/RCAF officers and 157 airmen.

The three FDT vessels that were tasked with controlling all RAF and USAAF air traffic during the assault were:

FDT-216 situated in the western half of the assault area beyond the American beaches of Omaha and Utah. FDT217

in the eastern half of the assault area off the British and Canadian beaches. This vessel was also designated as the Master Control FDT and had the additional role of managing fighter resources across the whole invasion area and FDT-13 positioned in the main shipping route to provide defensive cover to the main shipping lanes.

On 5 June, at 22:00 all three set sail from Cowes (on the Isle of Wight) to join the overall Assault Task Force and were in position by 04:30 on 6 June. To surprise the enemy as much as possible, the assault force approached the beaches under complete radio silence. All the FDTs switched on their radars at H-Hour, 07:25, and immediately took control of the fighter aircraft providing the defensive air umbrella.

The three FDTs continued their duty in the days after the initial invasion, returning to port periodically for re-supply. Because there was virtually no enemy activity within the main shipping channels, FDT-13 was moved closer to shore to track enemy mine laying and torpedo aircraft around the Cherbourg peninsular. She was replaced on 27 June by FDT-216 who then moved up the coast to Le Havre. At 00:59 on 7 July FDT-216 was hit by torpedo fired from a Junkers JU88 and capsized. All but five of her crew were rescued.

FDT-217 and FDT-13 both survived the war.

HMS FDT-216 was a British Royal Navy Fighter Direction Tender. Originally built by the US Navy and commissioned as HMS LST-216 in 1943, she was re-commissioned on 13 February 1944. She was sunk by enemy JU-88 aircraft-launched torpedo 23 miles west of Le Havre, France on 7 July 1944.

Air Surveillance and Control D-Day.

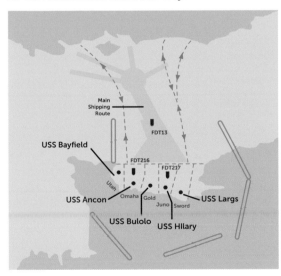

HQ Ships - assault Control

Air Corridors to and from assault areas

Night fighter patrol lines

A tough job

Crew on board the FDT vessels endured much hardship during their operation. The radar personnel had been on these vessels for several months, living in cramped accommodation intended only for tank crews on short transit trips. There was no air conditioning and the work areas were overcrowded. With a lack of exits, they were widely considered to be 'floating death traps'. Working continuous shifts of four hours on and four hours off in such poor conditions imposed a serious strain on the personnel and crew members

59 Operation PLUTO: Pipeline Under The Ocean

The Allied invasion force was one of the most mobile in history. The initial plan was to land no less than 14,000 vehicles on to the beaches on day one alone! By D-Day+12 there would be almost 100,000 Allied vehicles in Normandy. Getting these tanks, trucks, jeeps and other vehicles on to the beaches in the first place was one problem; keeping them running during the breakout and subsequent advance was an entirely different proposition. Once the army had landed in France it would need to be fed with millions of gallons of fuel and if the invasion was to be successful, the planners at SHAEF needed to work out a way of supplying the invasion force with a safe and plentiful supply of fuel for their vehicles and machines.

The obvious solution was to run a fleet of tankers between the south coast of England and France; however, these would be very susceptible to both Luftwaffe and U-Boat attack, as well as being overly dependent on the weather. Another way needed to be found.

The idea of an underwater pipe supplying fuel to the continent had been under discussion for several years but actually building it was easier said than done. Experiments in early 1943 with a short pipeline across the Bristol Channel revealed numerous challenges and operational issues and it took one hundred days before any fuel flowed

through – but it proved the concept and actively supplied elements of the Royal Army Service Corps and the Royal Engineers, based in Devon and Cornwall, with fuel.

In an effort to keep the large fuel storage facilities out of the Luftwaffe's reach, it was decided to store the fuel in places such as Bristol and Liverpool, rather than the south coast. This meant that before the Channel pipeline could be built, an extra 1,000 miles of inland pipeline was needed to transport the fuel to the south coast.

The main PLUTO operation consisted of over 70 miles of pipeline running from the Isle of Wight to the Cherbourg Peninsula. Construction started on 12 August 1944 and the first line was completed within a matter of weeks, supplying both British and American forces. However, the Allied forces were advancing quickly and almost immediately another PLUTO was needed from the Kent coast to Boulogne. This new line was laid in October 1944 with further lines laid over the coming months. In all, over 750 miles of pipeline were laid under the Channel with the sole purpose of delivering fuel to the Allied war machine.

By VE Day, over 170 million gallons of fuel had been delivered to the Allied forces. It was, quite simply, an incredible feat of ingenuity and engineering.

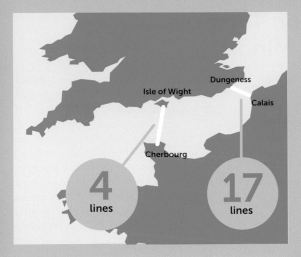

Isle of Wight

Dungeness

Calais

Cherbourg

4 lines

17 lines

305 tonnes of fuel per day

January 1945

3,048 tonnes of fuel per day

March 1945

It has been estimated that PLUTO carried approx.

173,000,000 gallons of fuel

Altogether there were

21 PLUTO lines covering

750 miles

Captain J.F. Hutchings, and Commander J.H. Lee, RNR, of Glasgow, Commanding Officer of HMS *Sanscroft*, watching the pipe being laid.

It took

600 men working across thirty-four naval vessels to lay the all the cables

60 Operation Tombola (PLUTO Minor)

Operation PLUTO (Pipeline Under The Ocean) was an amazing concept, but in reality it was not up and running until 12 August 1944 – some ten weeks after the initial landings. Regardless of the genius of PLUTO, it could be argued that it had little or no material effect on the supply of fuel and lubricants to the Allies during the Normandy campaign. Another programme of fuel delivery was needed to help get the invasion forces off the beaches and into France in the days immediately after the landings.

During D-Day the British shipped ashore 63,000 gallons of fuel to enable them to establish a beachhead and move inland. By 12 June this stockpile had increased to north of a million gallons. But with fuel consumption for motorised transport in the order of 1,000 tonnes a day, this stockpile would not last long. Another plan was needed to feed the Allied war machine while PLUTO was being put together.

To satisfy such huge fuel requirements, four ship-to-shore pipelines were set up and laid in both the Eastern and Western Task Force areas to enable tankers to offload their liquid cargo from offshore moorings directly into storage tanks in France. For the British, these storage facilities were based at Port-en-Bessin, while the Americans situated their fuel storage depot a few miles down the coast at Sainte-Honorine-des-Pertes.

Codenamed 'Tombola', each pipeline enabled a large tanker to discharge 600 tonnes of fuel per hour.

Tombola was relatively simple to set up and used 6-inch American standard seamless steel pipe sections which were joined together before being hauled out to sea and positioned on the seabed via a large wooden sledge. A heavy flexible pipe was attached to the sea end once it had been fixed in place. Moorings were put in place out to sea to enable tankers to haul up the flexible pipe and connect it to their own system and so pump the fuel ashore. The system was fully live within eighteen days of the first landings.

Operation Tombola allowed tankers to discharge up to

600

tonnes of fuel per hour

The Allies used German POWs to fill thousands of jerrycans each day for use in the field

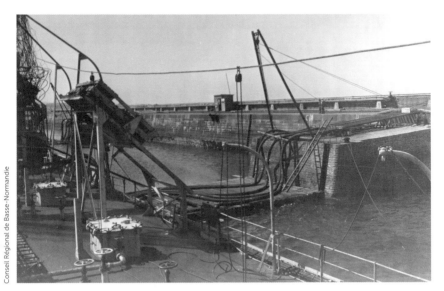

The ship to shore pipeline at Port-en-Bessin and following the road.

The pipeline running along a roadside at Bateau.

Operation Tombola was up and running after only eighteen days – almost a month before the main PLUTO lines were operational

61 Mulberry

If the liberation of Europe was to be successful, the Allies would need more than fuel. They would need to be able to reinforce the initial landings with hundreds of thousands more men and vehicles, along with the rations, ammunition and supplies needed to keep the army advancing in good order. The only major port close to the invasion beaches was Cherbourg, but there was no guarantee that this port could be utilised. They had to come up with a different solution.

On 30 May 1942 Churchill sent a note to Admiral Lord Louis Mountbatten, the Chief of Combined Operations:

Piers for use on the beaches
CCO or deputy

They must float up and down
with the tide.
The anchor problem must
be mastered.
Let me have the best
solution worked out.
Don't argue the matter.
The difficulties will argue
for themselves.

In September 1943, the idea for a floating harbour was agreed and ratified by the Combined Chiefs of Staff. The specifications required were formidable to say the least. There would be two harbours built, codenamed Mulberrys. Mulberry A for the Americans would be positioned at St Laurent, whereas Mulberry B for the British would be positioned at Arromanches. Three weeks after the first wave of the invasion force had landed in France, it was expected that each harbour needed to be capable of unloading 12,000 tonnes of cargo and 2,500 vehicles of varying size and design a day. Not only that, they would have to cope with the traffic of large ships, give shelter for landing craft in times of bad weather and be ready and fully operational by 1 May 1944.

Mountbatten and his team had just seven months to design and build two artificial harbours, each one the size of Dover.

Eventually the designers settled on building breakwaters (codenamed Gooseberries) using sunken ships. About seventy ships would be used for each Mulberry. Intermingled within these ships were a number of huge boxes of concrete (known as Phoenixes), some of these the size of a three-storey building.

Once these concrete Phoenix caissons were fixed, floating roadways were put in position, made up of steel pontoon bridges (codenamed Whales) that would be capable of moving in harmony with the 23-foot Normandy tide, enabling supplies to get ashore with minimum fuss.

During the ten months after D-Day, British Mulberry Harbour (Mulberry B) successfully brought ashore enormous amounts of reinforcements, armour and supplies:

2,500,000
men

500,000
vehicles

4,000,000
tonnes of equipment and rations

View of Omaha Beach following emplacement of the Gooseberry breakwater of sunken ships, c. mid-June 1944.

Construction began in the summer of 1943 and employed over

45,000
people across 300 engineering companies

2
million tons of steel and concrete used to build cassions

The harbours were a major work of civil engineering. 146 concrete caissons, each 60 metres long, 18 metres high and 15 metres wide made up 6 miles of breakwater. They were airtight floating cases open at the bottom with air-cocks to lower them to the seabed in a controlled fashion.

The concrete cassions were towed into position and sunk to make the harbours

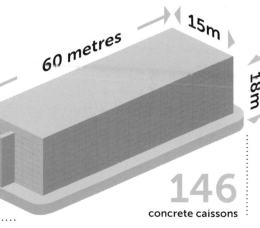

60 metres

15m

18m

146
concrete caissons

62 The Sherman DD (Duplex Drive) Tank

The concept of a 'swimming tank' goes back to the end of World War 1, when a floating version of the British Mark IX tank was tested in November 1918 – albeit without success. Throughout the inter-war years development continued. It was generally accepted that a tank powered by a secondary outboard motor 'swam' quite well; the biggest issue was designing a sensible flotation system that did not add too much bulk or size to the original tank. Many different ideas were tried and tested but it was not until Hungarian-born engineer Nicholas Straussler came up with his ingenious canvas screen in 1940 that the whole idea of the swimming tank gained serious credibility within the British War Office.

Initial trials were carried out using the Tetrach light tank in June 1941 at the Brent Reservoir in north London, with sea trials at Portsmouth following on quickly. Prototype construction concentrated on the reliable Valentine tank that was already in service and after further trials took place in May 1942, the Ministry of Supply placed an order the following month. However, by 1944 the Valentine tank had been largely superseded by the American built M4 Sherman, which was used by all the major Allied armies at the time. As well as being a more modern tank, the Sherman also had one distinct advantage that made it a better candidate for being a combat-ready amphibious tank – it could 'swim' ashore with its gun pointing

forward, ready to fight as soon as it hit land.

Converting the M4 Sherman consisted of a folding screen that was attached to a collapsible tubular metal frame secured to the tank's hull above the running gear. Compressed gas was used to inflate thirty-six rubber tubes that raised the screen and metal frame into position, where it was manually locked into place. It took eight minutes to inflate the screen, which extended up 7 foot, by which time the tank displaced enough water to float. The screen was also tall enough to hide the tank from view. To enemy observers it would look like a small canvas boat.

Because of the transmission design of the M4 Sherman,. A secondary drive system was needed to power the propellers; hence the tank being known as the Sherman DD or Sherman Duplex Drive.

While at sea the driver used a small rudder to steer, although he needed a periscope to be able to see where he was going. Once ashore, the canvas screen was simply discarded.

The Sherman DD was used to equip American, British and Canadian forces for the D-Day landings and saw action on all five landing zones. Never before had tanks supported the infantry so early in an amphibious assault. DDs were carried towards the shoreline in a Landing Craft,

Tank (LCT) with a plan to be launched into the Channel around 2 miles out. On the whole the DD tanks performed well on D-Day, despite the rough weather which resulted in sea conditions much worse than any they had been tested in. However, those tanks that did manage to swim ashore provided significant armoured and moral support to the infantry. This success resulted in them being utilised for further amphibious operations, including the crossing of the Rhine in 1945.

On D-Day,

176

tanks were launched:

At Omaha Beach 27 out of the 29 tanks launched sank in rough seas

In the run up to D-Day over

30,000

test launches were conducted as part of the DD tanks training

121

made it to shore

Crew:

5

Weight: 31.29 tons
Max speed road: 25 mph
Max speed water: 4 knots
Engine output: 375 bhp

Folded screen raises for amphibious use

63 Assault Vehicle Royal Engineers (AVRE)

The disastrous Dieppe Raid of 19 August 1942 forced a great deal of re-evaluating as to how combat engineers would operate on the battlefield. During the Dieppe operation engineers were tasked with getting the tanks off the beach, destroying obstacles and building ramps, but they quikly became a priority target for the defending German forces and suffered very high casualty rates. With tanks unable to leave the beaches, the raid stalled and failed.

An Officer of the Royal Canadian Engineers, John James Denovan, who was attached to the Special Devices Branch of the Department of Tank Design, used this experience and began work on developing an armoured vehicle that would support Engineers during assault operations.

Denovan based his design on the current Churchill infantry tank. Working with Lieutenant Colonel George Reeves, who had been an observer at the Raid on Dieppe, the first thing they decided to do with the standard Churchill was completely strip out the inside and build large equipment and storage areas to hold explosives, charges, fuses and various other pieces of equipment essential for Royal Engineer operations. They then decided to give it a gun powerful enough to destroy targets without getting out of the tank. This gun needed to be able to destroy concrete strong points or blow a large hole in any obstacle they came across and so Denovan chose a spigot mortar that could fire a huge 40lb (18.4kg) Petard mortar, known as 'the flying dustbin' due to their size.

The vehicle in testing was known as the Assault Vehicle Royal Engineers (AVRE) and following successful trials, production started in early 1944. The AVREs would be based on the Mk.III and IV Churchill and were assigned to three regiments of the Royal Engineers, forming the new 1st Assault Brigade Royal Engineers, part of the 79th Armoured Division.

A total of 754 Churchill III and IV tanks were converted to AVRE specification during the war, with the majority being used by Major General Sir Percy Hobart's 79th Armoured Division. On D-Day AVRE vehicles were successfully used to breach defences in the Atlantic Wall and proved valuable to the Allied advance. They were used in the D-Day landings and continued to be in use through the rest of the Allied advance to Nazi Germany.

The Fascine

A bundle of wooden poles or rough brushwood lashed together with wires carried in front of the tank that could be released to fill a ditch or form a step

The Small Box Girder

An assault bridge that was carried in front of the tank and could be dropped to span a 30-foot (9.1-metre) gap in thirty seconds

The Bullshorn Plough

A mine plough intended to excavate the ground in front of the tank, to expose and make harmless any land mines

The Bobbin

A reel of 10-foot (3.0-metre) wide canvas cloth reinforced with steel poles carried in front of the tank and unrolled onto the ground to form a 'path', so that following vehicles (and the deploying vehicle itself) would not sink into the soft ground of the beaches during the amphibious landing

Mk.IV Churchill AVRE

Weight: 39,600 kg

Max speed: 27 km/h

Range: 144 km

Engine output: 350 bhp

Crew: 5

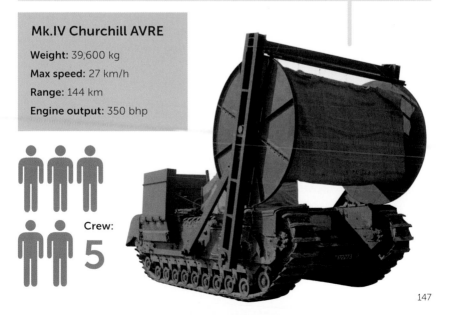

64 The Sherman Crab

During World War 2, both sides laid millions of anti-personnel and anti-tank mines – posing serious threat to advancing columns of vehicles and men. Dozens of different ways of dealing with such mines were considered but precious few ever made it past the prototype stage.

One idea that did have support was the idea of a mine flail. A device, made up of heavy chains ending in a ball of steel (flails) roughly the size of a fist, that was mounted to the front of an armoured vehicle. The device would then spin rapidly, causing the flails to smash into the ground, causing any mines nearby to detonate.

Early development work resulted in twenty-five Matilda tanks being adapted with a revolving flail drum for use in the Second Battle of El Alamein. Although these modified Matildas were quite effective at mine clearing they broke down regularly and the flail system was not reliable, meaning much of the mine clearing had to be done the old-fashioned way – by hand.

Development of the flail concept continued, with further designs being based on the British Valentine tank and the American M4 A4 Sherman. It was one of the Sherman designs – the Sherman Crab – that eventually went into full production.

The Crab's rotor carried forty-three flails and was driven at 142 rpm by a driveshaft running down the right-hand side of the tank. An extra gearbox was added to maintain the correct flail speed when the tank was travelling slower, such as when climbing a hill. Other innovations that made it on to the Crab included the addition of cutters to the rotor that proved very effective at tearing up barbed wire, a counterweighted jib that kept the rotor at the right height, ensuring mines buried in a dip would not be missed, and a blast shield that provided added crew protection from exploding mines.

Crabs also carried a pair of bins filled with powdered chalk that slowly trickled out to mark the edges of the safe route. The crew could also drop smoke grenades and illuminated poles out of a hopper.

The Sherman Crab had its first taste of combat on D-Day when three flail regiments went ashore as part of the 30th Armoured Brigade, 79th Armoured Division. When flailing, the Crab could only move at a sedate 1.25 mph (2km/h) and had to have its gun pointing to the rear meaning it could not properly defend itself. That said, it proved to be an effective and valuable machine during D-Day and the subsequent advance through western Europe.

By spring 1945 the threat of minefields had all but disappeared and it was suggested that any surviving Crabs be converted back to regular Sherman tanks. Such a move was strongly challenged by the Crab crews who didn't want to return to 'normal tanks'. In the end this did not happen, and the Crabs saw out the war clearing old minefields within Allied territory.

Alamy

A Sherman crab flail tank under test, 79th Armoured Division, 27 April 1944.

'I ran slap-bang into an 88-millimetre gun emplacement which didn't take long to neutralise my tank. I was hit twice: one up the side and into the engine and one on the turret. The next thing we knew, we were standing in flames. The whole tank burst into flames. The only I could do was swing the turret round to make sure the driver and the co-driver could get out and I shouted, "Bail out!" and we bailed out. I went along the sand dune and there was another tank from another squadron and the commander had been sniped through the head. I came behind the tank and I shouted, "Shove him out!" They shoved the body out and I got into the tank and went on'

Corporal George Sidney Kenneth Agnew, flail tank commander, 22 Dragoons

The Crab could only move at

1.25

miles per hour (2 km/h) when flailing, and the gun had to point to the rear, so the tank could not fire even if the gunner could see his target

65 The Churchill Crocodile

From the very beginning of the war there had been significant interest and experimentation regarding the fitting of flamethrowers on to British armoured vehicles. Development work between the Petroleum Warfare Department and the Ministry of Supply, resulted in a demonstration of an early Churchill tank prototype in 1943, Major General Sir Percy Hobart liked what he saw and lobbied the Ministry of Supply to consider production for the 79th Armoured Division – which it duly did.

The flamethrower element of the Crocodile was produced as a kit which could be retrospectively fitted to any Churchill Mk.VII in the field. The kit consisted of a two-wheeled armoured trailer for the fuel, an armoured pipe that ran underneath the tank and the hull-mounted projector, which replaced the tank's BESA machine-gun.

The armoured trailer weighed in at six-and-a-half-tonnes and could carry 400 imperial gallons of fuel plus five cylinders of compressed gas propellant. The trailer was connected to the tank via an armoured coupling which could be released from inside the tank if required. For covering long distances, the trailers were towed by trucks, but with no suspension or brakes this was a more tricky than it seemed.

The flamethrower itself had a range of around 100 metres and used a fuel that was a mixture of petrol, oil and rubber which made a viscous, sticky substance that stuck to any surface with which it came into contact. Initially it was designed to attack concrete strong points but was equally adept at clearing woodland and built up areas. The fuel mixture would even burn on water – nowhere was safe from the Churchill Crocodile. There was enough fuel in the tanks for eighty one-second bursts of fire, or a series of bursts of longer duration if needed. Before they could fire anything, the crew had to prime the system, which took about 15 minutes before reaching optimum operation pressure. This optimum pressure could not be maintained for very long, however, so crews had to prime the system as close to the front line as possible.

During D-Day only a handful of Crocodiles actually made it ashore in one piece. However, once the battle for Normandy started the Crocodiles came into their own. Used by specialist units of the 79th Armoured Division, the Crocodile was an effective assault weapon that could (and often did) induce the surrender of large numbers of enemy troops with just one or two bursts of flame. Indeed, the flamethrower was so reviled by the Germans that any captured Crocodile crews were often executed.

Overall some 800 kits were produced, with around 250 kits kept in reserve for operations in the Far East. However, in the end it was decided that the terrain would be too rough for the trailer and they were not deployed.

WikiCommons

Churchill Crocodile Tank on display outside the D-Day Museum at Southsea.

Top secret mechanism

Aspects of the mechanism were considered by the British to be so secret that disabled units, if they could not be recovered, were rapidly destroyed by any means possible, including air strike

'One of the navy men had a big pole with markings on it. He dipped the water at each side of this ramp and said, "Right, No 1 tank off." He went off, straight forward, sunk. The crew got out, left the tank, swam back. No 2 went out, turned to the left, he went down. There was ten tanks on and No 3 went to the right and he went straight through on to the beach so the said, "Right, follow him." We left them, them two tanks. You couldn't do nowt about them'

Trooper Joseph Ellis, Churchill Crocodile Driver, 141st Regiment, Royal Armoured Corps

Fuel carried: 400 imperial gallons (1,800 litres)

Operation pressure: 600psi

Flamethrower range: 120 yards (110 m)

Fuel useage: 4 imperial gallons per second (18 litres per second)

Numbers of kits built: Approximately

800

66 The Airspeed Horsa glider

It takes a certain type of bravery to enter a war zone, behind enemy lines, in an aircraft largely made from wood or canvas and without engines, but that is exactly how many British and American toops went into battle on D-Day.

On 12 October 1940, the Ministry of Aircraft Production issued Specification X.26/40 for a military assault glider capable of carrying twenty-five troops and two crew. One of the companies to submit a design was Airspeed Ltd, a subsidiary of de Havilland Aircraft Co. who submitted a design called the Horsa. On 12 September 1941 the first prototype Horsa (DG597) was towed aloft from the Great West Aerodrome at Hounslow (now Heathrow Airport) by an Armstrong Whitworth Whitley. By this time an order of several hundred Horsas had already been placed by the British Government and production of the Airspeed Horsa commenced in earnest in early 1942. By May the order book had grown to almost 2,500 units.

As requested, the Horsa could carry twenty-five troops plus a crew of two. Alternatively, a six-pounder gun and its tow jeep plus the gun crew could be accommodated. Heavy equipment, such as the gun or jeep was unloaded by either detonating a small explosive charge to blow off the rear fuselage or, if time permitted, the tail section could be unbolted from the main fuselage with a spanner. Far from satisfactory, the Airspeed designers were forced to come up with a better solution and the Horsa Mk.II boasted a hinged nose to allow vehicles and artillery pieces a much easier route on and off the glider.

The Horsa's military debut was nothing short of disastrous. On the night of 19/20 November 1942 two gliders took part in the unsuccessful attack on the German heavy water plant at Rjukan in Norway. Both gliders crashed in bad weather and all twenty-three survivors were executed on the orders of Adolf Hitler.

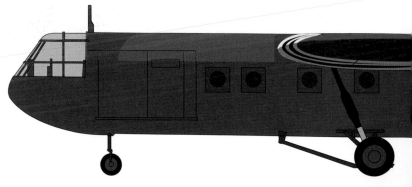

The first large-scale deployment of Horsa gliders was on 10 July 1943 during Operation Husky, the Allied invasion of Sicily. Eleven months later, six Horsas carried men from the British 6 Airborne Division as they made their way towards their objectives of two road bridges crossing the River Orne and Caen Canal in the opening salvo of the D-Day invasion. Hundreds of Horsas were subsequently involved in the large-scale British airborne operation (Operation Tonga) that took place between 5 and 7 June as part of the wider D-Day landings.

Around 3,800 Horsa gliders were built in total, with over 300 being used by American forces.

'We heard the glider pilot shout, "Casting off!" and suddenly the roar of the aeroplane engine receded and we were in a silent world. It was like being trapped in a floating coffin in mid-space'

**Private Harry Clark,
24 Platoon, D Company,
2 Battalion, Ox and Bucks
Light Infantry**

**Numbers built
Mk.I & Mk.II**

3,799

Capacity:
25 troops or six pounder anti-tank gun plus towing jeep and ammunition

Length: 67 ft 0 in (20.43 m)
Wingspan: 88 ft 0 in (26.83 m)
Height: 19 ft 6 in (5.95 m)

Crew:

2

LF912

Speed: 150 mph (242 km/h) on tow
100 mph (160 km/h) gliding

67 Operation Tiger

By June 1943 the decision had been made to use Normandy as the landing zone for the invasion. SHAEF considered major training exercises essential and Slapton Sands, situated some 10 miles down the coast from Torquay, was chosen for the training – its steep shingle beaches closely resembling the beaches of Normandy, especially Omaha and Utah. Other sites towards the east of Portsmouth were used to help the British simulate the landings that would take place on Gold, Juno and Sword beaches. On the evening of 26 April, troops boarded several Landing Ship, Tank (LST) vessels and set sail. In an attempt to simulate crossing the English Channel the ships took a wide route around Lyme Bay so they could arrive back on Slapton Sands at first light the following morning. The landings would be preceded by a live fire exercise to get the men accustomed to the sight, sound and smell of gunfire – on paper it would be a perfect practise run for the invasion proper.

The initial plan was for the heavy cruiser HMS *Hawkins* to shell the beach with live ammunition from 06:30 to 07:00, with the landings taking place at 07:30 after beachmasters had inspected the landing area to ensure it was safe. However, a number of the LSTs were late in their approach to Slapton so the officer in command decided to postpone the landings by one hour to 08:30. The live firing exercise would also be delayed by an hour. This new order was received by

HMS *Hawkins* but not by all of the LSTs, some of which approached the beach at the original time of 07:30 – just as the live firing started. Even though the beach was cordoned off by white tape to stop men crossing during the firing, many soldiers ignored the tape and carried on. Hundreds of men were killed or wounded.

At 09:45 on 27 April, a convoy of five LSTs sailed from Plymouth bound for Slapton, accompanied by the Flower-class corvette HMS *Azalea*. The convoy was joined by three more LSTs as it passed Torbay before heading northwest towards Slapton Sands. They were completely oblivious to the fact that nine German E-boats of the 5th and 9th Schnellboote flotillas had managed to slip past British motor torpedo boats (MTBs) and were patrolling the area looking for likely targets.

At 23:17 the 5th flotilla was sent bearings of a possible target from their command base in Cherbourg. The six E-boats of the flotilla split into pairs as they started the hunt. At around 01:30 the convoy had been discovered, within a few minutes LST 507 and LST 531 had been sunk and two others had been badly damaged. In the confusion Allied Commanders ordered all remaining vessels to scatter, but the order left many men floating in the cold sea to die of hypothermia.

639 men were killed in the E-boat attack, with hundreds more wounded. In total, the Operation Tiger death toll has been put at 946 men

'I remember being on the navigation deck of the ship when the radar man pointed out a "little peep" on the corner of the radar screen. I went out to take a look and was standing on the starboard wing when the first torpedo hit. It felt like a sledgehammer on my feet. It threw me back eight or nine feet.

Ensign Douglas Harlander, LST 531 Navigation Officer

A disastrous secret

To the outside world, the disaster of Operation Tiger (also known as Exercise Tiger) was kept a closely guarded secret. No official communiqué was issued and the staff of the local Sherbourne Hospital in Dorset, who received hundreds of hypothermia and burns cases, were told to ask no questions and warned that they would be subject to court martial if they discussed the tragedy

Sea rescue

Captain John Doyle, of LST 515, the lead ship of the convoy, disobeyed orders and returned to rescue survivors from the sea. His crew rescued approximately 134 men that would have surely perished

American troops landing on Slapton Sands in England during rehearsals for the invasion of Normandy.

68 Operation Bodyguard

One of the biggest considerations that the invasion planners had to think about was how they could hide the actual location and date of the invasion from the Germans. And so was christened Operation Bodyguard.

Operation Bodyguard would be the most elaborate, the most intricate and the most daring military bluff ever undertaken. If it worked, it would be simply beautiful. If it failed, the men landing on the beaches of Normandy in the summer of 1944 would be walking headlong into a whole world of trouble. There was no option. It had to work.

The entire ruse needed to achieve three separate deceptions:

1. **Disguise the geographical point of the invasion.**

2. **Confuse the enemy as to when the landings would take place.**

3. **Finally, it had to try and convince the Germans that the actual full-scale invasion was in fact a diversion and the 'real' invasion force would be landing somewhere else.**

Because they could monitor German encrypted communications, SHAEF knew that the Germans were expecting the main attack to be aimed at the Pas-de-Calais, so it made sense for a large

chunk of the Bodyguard bluff to keep this illusion alive in the minds of the enemy. To this end, a huge sub-campaign was launched called Operation Fortitude. To make Fortitude South credible, a huge ghost army, the First US Army Group (FUSAG) was built, and in an effort to give it further credibility, it was given a real life (and suitably high-profile) commander in the shape of US General George S. Patton. The Allies even created authentic army radio traffic that was purposefully made easy to decipher which made numerous references to a planned invasion.

To add to the bluff, thousands of dummy planes, tanks, guns, and jeeps were fabricated. The 'make believe' vehicles and equipment were not perfect replicas, and were obviously dummies if viewed up close, but when viewed from a German reconnaissance aircraft they looked like the real deal. Leaks to the press added to the reality of FUSAG and some of Britain's finest architects were employed to create a huge but completely fake oil dock at Dover. The RAF patrolled constantly over the area as if they were protecting it and when it was hit by enemy bombs, fires were started by lighting massive sodium flares.

At the same time as the deception in the south, another operation, nicknamed Fortitude North kicked off in Scotland. This operation mirrored Fortitude South in so much as there was another fantasy army in place, this one being positioned and primed to 'invade' the coasts of Denmark and Norway. No physical dummies were created for Fortitude North, as the Allies decided that enemy planes would not get so far north without being intercepted by the RAF. Instead, this operation relied on mis-information being delivered to the enemy via false radio traffic and double agents. In the end though, Fortitude North failed to goad to much of a reaction out of the Germans.

The final act of Operation Bodyguard was played out on D-Day itself. Hitler and his staff were convinced that the Pas-de-Calais would be the destination of choice for the invasion party and as such refused to release reinforcements to help out in Normandy for several hours after the landings. By the time Hitler realised there would be no second invasion, the Allies had managed to get ashore and were building up forces quickly to meet the expected enemy counter-attack.

The greatest bluff in military history had worked beautifully.

Soldiers lift up and position an inflatable rubber tank dummy as part of Operation Fortitude.

Did you know?

Operation Bodyguard was approved on Christmas Day 1943. The new name had been chosen based on a comment made by Winston Churchill to Joseph Stalin at the Tehran conference: 'In wartime, truth is so precious that she should always be attended by a bodyguard of lies'

'As yet there is no immediate prospect of the invasion'

Field Marshal von Rundstedt, situation report, 5 June 1944

69 Operation Ironside

Operation Bodyguard would never had been as successful as it was if it had not been for the network of agents and double agents that drip-fed the enemy with information and mis-information in the months running up to the invasion in a brazen attempt to confuse and deceive. In another sub-campaign to Bodyguard (Operation Ironside), the Allies wanted to amplify German concerns about a potential invasion around the Bay of Biscay. The navy and the air force could not provide any resource to help create a physical deception, so it decided to run the entire campaign through double agents, with Bronx, a South American socialite and agent with ties to Vichy France, leading the operation.

Bronx refused to use radios when in England due to safety concerns; instead she wrote letters to the Germans. Over time she sent over sixty letters to the enemy, and became highly trusted; however, the Germans realised that if, through her social circles, Bronx picked up any information concerning D-Day, the letters would arrive too late to be of any use. Instead, they devised a code system based on a seemingly innocent telegram that would be sent to the General Manager of the Bank of Espírito Santo in Madrid, a bank with strong links to the Deutsche Bank. The code described various areas of the French coast through different monetary values. If the money was requested for the dentists, it would indicate the

information was certain; if the telegram mentioned a doctor, this would mean the information was less certain. If Bronx requested the money to be sent 'straight away', this would indicate that the invasion would take place in less than a week. Urgent meant within two weeks; 'quickly' suggested the invasion would happen within a month; whereas the term 'if possible' meant the exact date was not known.

On 29 May 1944, just a week before D-Day, Bronx sent a coded telegram that managed to get the attention of senior German officers:

Send £50 immediately.
I need it for my dentist.

The £50 indicated that the place of invasion was the Bay of Biscay, by using the word 'immediately' told the Germans the invasion was expected in the next week and the fact the money was for the dentist meant the information was certain. The telegram was backed up by a letter, dated 7 June, although the Germans would not have received that letter for several weeks. In the letter Bronx explained that she got talking to a captain at a party and he told her that there was going to be an airborne assault in the Bordeaux area that night in preparation for an invasion. However, the next morning the captain had contacted Bronx and admitted that the invasion had been delayed.

The result? To be truthful, German intelligence never really truly believed that the invasion would come in the Bay of Biscay area and it seems that they regarded most rumours of any such landings as nothing more than cover operation. That being said, there were two main panzer divisions located in the Bay of Biscay area; following the invasion only the 17th SS Panzer Division moved north to intercept – and they were delayed by a number of days. Meanwhile, the 11th Panzer Division remained in situ to guard the region. On this basis it could be said that, if nothing else, Operation Ironside added to the overall confusion for German commanders and helped to slow down their decision-making. The delay in releasing the panzers gave the invasion forces a vital window of relative safety in which to establish a beachhead.

'By means of the double agent system, we actively ran and controlled the German espionage system in this country'

Sir John Cecil Masterman OBE

Sir John Cecil Masterman OBE

When World War 2 broke out, Masterman was drafted into the Intelligence Corps where he was appointed as a Civil Assistant in the MI5. Within MI5 he became chairman of the Twenty Committee, a group of British Intelligence officials who ran the 'Double Cross' system, turning German spies into double agents

The 'Double Cross' System

Agent Bronx was one of five double agents feeding false information to the Germans in the run-up to D-Day. They were part of the 'Double Cross' system operated by the Twenty Committee. It was called 'Double Cross' because the number twenty in Roman numerals (XX) forms a double cross

70 Combined bomber offensive

The Germans had long known that any Allied invasion would be prefaced by an intense and widespread air attack on inland communication and railway systems. Yet, without an effective air force of their own, they also knew that when the attack came, they would be practically powerless to do anything about it.

In the field, Generalfeldmarschall von Rundstedt did not have enough motor vehicles even for his front-line forces and had to rely almost entirely on the rail network for supplies. By 1944 the French railway system was a shadow of its pre-war self – the campaign of 1940 had seen thousands of railway stations and ancillary buildings destroyed and the subsequent German occupation saw 4,000 locomotives, 31,000 passenger wagons and almost half a million freight wagons moved out to Germany. Even before a single Allied bomb fell in 1944, the French rail network was severely strained and plagued by active sabotage and passive resistance from both the local workforce and the French Resistance.

The initial plan to attack several pre-selected rail routes in the run up to D-Day was drawn up in late 1943 but was rejected by Air Chief Marshal Sir Trafford Leigh-Mallory because he could not guarantee the required machinery and manpower so close to the invasion. As an alternative, the AEAF (Allied Expeditionary Air Force) developed a plan for a three-month bombing campaign against carefully selected targets across France and Belgium in an effort to disrupt rail traffic in and out of the invasion area. The official directive to commence the bombing was issued by General Eisenhower on 17 April 1944.

Three separate air force units were used for the bombing: targets in eastern France and parts of Belgium were allocated to the US Eighth Air Force; RAF Bomber Command was given targets in western France and Paris; and a combined AEAF group was ordered to attack targets throughout northern France and Belgium. Although no German targets were officially approved as part of the plan, the US Eighth Air Force dropped about 5,000 tonnes of bombs on rail centres within Germany.

Initial sorties were productive with almost all targets hit and German repair teams were struggling to keep up with the rate of destruction. In May, the intensity of the attacks were stepped up and key bridges were added to the list of targets, including bridges over the Seine, Oise and Meuse rivers. The attacks on the bridges were spectacularly successful. By the end of the month all routes over the Seine north of Paris were closed to motorised traffic and remained closed until well after the invasion. German repairs were closely monitored and when it was clear that a bridge was close to being re-opened to traffic, it was attacked once again. Overall, the bombing raids on the rail network reduced effective rail traffic in France by 60 per cent in the month before D-Day and severely hampered the German Army's ability to resist the invasion.

On D-Day itself there were 171 RAF and USAF squadrons in the air supporting the invasion through a variety of tasks and objectives. Some stayed out at sea to provide cover to the invasion fleet, while others attacked the fortifications of the Atlantic Wall to reduce the enemy firepower on to the various landing zones. German radar stations from Le Havre to Barfleur were also attacked, so that the invading armada could approach the Normandy coastline undetected. Results were mixed; the attacks on the radar stations were very effective with over seventy stations destroyed, but the low cloud levels meant that bombing coastal fortifications proved to be quite tricky – indeed, many sorties were cancelled due to poor weather conditions.

Pre-invasion bombing of Pointe du Hoc by 9th Air Force bombers.

'For a month, probably two months, we were operating against German radar stations with rockets and bombs but mostly rockets. Our job was to eliminate the German radar in the Channel with the exception of two stations which were deliberately left in order to spoof the invasion'

Group Captain Denys Gillam, 146 Wing, RAF

On the night of 5/6 June, Bomber Command flew

1,211 sorties

During the 6 June D-Day assault itself, a total of 171 squadrons of British and AAF fighters undertook a variety of tasks in support of the invasion. Fifteen squadrons provided shipping cover, fifty-four provided beach cover, thirty-three undertook bomber escort and offensive fighter sweeps, thirty-three struck at targets inland from the landing area, and thirty-six provided direct air support to invading forces

71 The most critical message of the day

At 02:51 the American command ship *Ancon* dropped anchor just 11 miles off Omaha beach. At about the same time Generalfeldmarschall von Rundstedt received a message from General Max Pemsel suggesting engine noise could be heard out in the Baie de Seine. On hearing the news, he instructed Colonel Bodo Zimmermann to contact Führerhauptquartier and tell them what was happening. Now was the time for von Rundstedt to act – he had received no forewarnings from the Luftwaffe, the Kriegsmarine or any radar operative, but he did still have one significant ace up his sleeve: the panzers.

If he could get the panzers moving up to the coast immediately, they would be in position to meet any invasion full on with minimal interference by Allied naval and air bombardments. Furthermore, the early morning mist would provide the perfect cloak to hide his armour as they moved into position. Quick and decisive positioning of the panzers could result in the invasion being pushed back into the sea before it even got started.

The trouble was, von Rundstedt did not command all of the panzers. Some were commanded by Rommel, others could not be moved without the direct say-so of Hitler himself. After some procrastination, von Rundstedt decided to act and ordered the 12th SS Panzer Division Hitler Jugend and the Panzer Lehr Division to move up to the Normandy coast immediately. Crucially, he then ordered half of the 12th SS Division armour to divert to a different part of the coast near Deauville in response to Allied dummy parachute drops.

After he had issued the relevant orders, he sent a message to OKW:

OB-WEST IS FULLY AWARE THAT IF THIS IS ACTUALLY A LARGE-SCALE ENEMY
OPERATION IT CAN ONLY BE MET SUCCESSFULLY IF IMMEDIATE ACTION IS
TAKEN. THIS INVOLVES THE COMMITMENT ON THIS DAY OF THE AVAILABLE
STRATEGIC RESERVES... THE 12TH SS AND THE PANZER LEHR DIVISIONS. IF
THEY ASSEMBLE QUICKLY AND GET AN EARLY START THEY CAN ENTER
THE BATTLE ON THE COAST DURING THE DAY.

Arguably, this was the most critical message of D-Day. If OKW had agreed to von Rundstedt's actions he would have been able to launch a significant counterattack that could quite possibly have changed the course of history.

Unfortunately, the staff members at OKW did not quite grasp the gravity of the situation. The news was not deemed important enough to disturb either Alfred Jodl (Oberkommando der Wehrmacht) or Hitler. When Jodl eventually woke and was told the news he was furious and immediately ordered members of his staff to call von Rundstedt and order him to halt the panzers and await Hitler's decision.

Thus, instead of having 500 tanks, 100 assault guns and around 40,000 panzer grenadiers at his disposal, von Rundstedt could only count on 146 tanks and 51 guns from the 21st Panzer Division.

It was not until after 14:00 that Hitler decided to allow von Rundstedt control of the Hitler Jugend and Panzer Lehr Divisions; however it was too little too late. The option of an immediate and decisive counterattack was lost.

'When we warned that if we didn't get the panzers the Normandy landings would succeed and that unforeseeable consequences would follow, we were simply told that we were in position to judge – that the main landing was going to come at an entirely different place anyway'

Colonel Bodo Zimmermann

Generalfeldmarschall von Rundstedt

72 Operation Neptune

A few hours after the decision to launch Operation Overlord, the invasion fleet was in final preparations to slip out to sea. Following pre-designated shipping lanes hundreds of vessels began to arrive at a naval assembly area just south of the Isle of Wight, which was fittingly called 'Piccadilly Circus'. It was here that the final checks were made, the timings and routes were confirmed and re-confirmed, and it was here where over 150,000 crew and men waited nervously for the nod to set sail towards the Normandy coast.

The huge armada of mine sweepers, destroyers, cruisers, troop ships and cargo ships made up Operation Neptune – the code name given to the assault phase of Operation Overlord – the larger plan for the liberation of northwest Europe.

Detailed planning for a major cross-Channel amphibious operation began in late April 1942 under the leadership of Admiral Sir Bertram Ramsay who was appointed as naval commander. Ramsay's plan was relatively simple on paper. It was assumed that the vast aerial power of the Allies would ensure that the fleet would be free from a German attack from the air. Therefore, the whole armada would be spear-headed by a flotilla of minesweepers that would clear the way for the ships behind them. They would be followed by the warships, whose job it would be to bombard the German beach defences prior to the invasion. The troop-carrying aspect of

the convoy would then move forward on to the shoreline and deposit the cargo of men and equipment as near to the beaches as possible. With a huge naval force boasting 6,939 vessels and some 195,000 men, it would be the largest amphibious invasion in history.

Once the Normandy coast had been chosen as the target for Operation Neptune, planning started on how to get the men and equipment ashore. Five different beach landing zones were identified named Sword, Juno, Gold, Omaha and Utah. The extreme flanks of the invasion zone and the area immediately inland from the beaches would be secured by airborne troops dropped in from the skies.

Omaha Beach, 6 June, ships of all shapes and size unloading while barrage balloons hover overhead

Adverse storms delayed the invasion until 6 June and, even then, the weather proved a tricky adversary, throwing up large waves and heavy swells all the way into the shoreline. Despite the rough journeys, over 130,000 men were put ashore on D-Day, with hundreds of thousands more to follow over the following few weeks, and millions of tonnes of equipment off-loaded via temporary harbours.

Operation Neptune officially came to an end on 30 June 1944 (D-Day+24). By this date, 570 Liberty Ships, 180 troop transports, 788 coasters and 905 LSTs, as well as 1,814 LCTs and LCI(L)s, had delivered their cargoes to the Normandy coastline, landing 861,838 men, 157,633 vehicles and 501,834 tons of equipment and supplies.

Neptune in numbers

6,939 vessels

1,213 naval warships

4,126 landing ships and craft

864 merchant ships **736** ancillary craft

195,700 personnel

52,889 United States

112,824 British

4,988 Other Allied countries

11,590 aircraft were available to support the invasion

A single division formed the initial assault force on each beach, reinforced by 'special service' units (Commandos or Rangers). The flanks were secured by pre-dawn landings by 6th (British) and 82nd and 101st (US) Airborne Divisions

After a frustrating night and day at anchor, the weather abated enough and on the evening of 5th June we were on our way. The flotilla set off around midnight, along with many other craft of all sizes. As dawn broke, we were one of many landing craft waiting off Sword Beach

John Dennett, Able Seaman, Royal Navy. HMS LST-322

73 The first shot – HMS *Warspite*

Many people, including her own crew, thought that the guns of HMS *Belfast* fired the opening salvo of the naval bombardment in the early morning of D-Day; however, this was not the case. Lieutenant Peter Brooke Smith, who was serving on board HMS *Belfast*, recorded in his diary that another cruiser to the west fired first at 05:23. The entry in HMS *Belfast's* log records that she opened fire three minutes later at 05:27, 'with full broadside to port'.

That cruiser to the west was, in fact, the battleship HMS *Warspite* and, at a distance of 26,000 yards, she had just started to pound the German battery at Villerville that overlooked Sword Beach. She was accompanied in her long-range assault by another battleship, HMS *Ramillies*, the monitor HMS *Roberts*, four cruisers and thirteen destroyers. It was a much heavier bombardment than originally planned in the draft plan of Operation Neptune, but with strong defences in this area, the commanders at SHAEF thought it was better to be safe than sorry. With the relative success of the Sword landing, those commanders could well sense their decision justified. Not long after *Warspite's* guns had announced the seaborne part of the invasion of Europe, overhead flew the second wave of gliders carrying soldiers of the British 6th Airborne Division. The battleship's Commanding Officer, Captain M.H.A. Kelsey drew the crew's attention to the spectacle by telling them over the broadcast system: 'All personnel not on full Action Stations can come up on deck to witness a sight you will never see again in your lifetime.'

She continued bombardment duties on 7 June, but after firing over 300 shells in just 48 hours she was forced to return to Portsmouth to re-arm. A quick turnaround saw her back in the action at Normandy on 9 June, supporting the American beachheads, especially around Omaha where troops were still having a hard time. *Warspite's* assistance was badly needed, as the US Navy's bombardment vessels, including the battleship USS *Arkansas,* were running short of shells.

Between 16:12 and 18:25, HMS *Warspite* fired ninety-six rounds, smashing a key enemy artillery position. On 11 June she took up position off Gold Beach to support the British 69th Infantry Brigade near Cristot before returning back to Portsmouth to re-arm the following day. Whilst at Portsmouth it was discovered that her guns were worn, so she was ordered to sail to Rosyth via the Straits of Dover for a re-fit. Early on 13 June, 28 miles off the coast of Harwich, she hit an enemy mine, which damaged her propeller shafts. The subsequent repairs kept her out of action until August, by which time the Admiralty considered her as mainly a bombardment vessel to attack enemy land-based defensive structures.

Once repaired, *Warspite* made her way down to the small island of Ushant, off the northwest coast of France and attacked the coastal batteries at Le Conquet and Pointe Saint-Mathieu during the Battle for Brest. By 10 September she had sailed north to carry out a preparatory bombardment of targets around Le Havre, prior to Operation Astonia, which led to the capture of the town within forty-eight hours. On 1 November her final task was to support an Anglo-Canadian operation around the port of Antwerp, which had been captured in September, by clearing the Scheldt Estuary of German strongholds and gun emplacements. This would be the last time she would fire her guns in action.

By the end of 1944 the war was beginning to take its toll on the 'Grand Old Lady', as she was affectionally known. On 1 January 1945, HMS *Warspite* was placed in reserve and then definitively retired from service. Although there were proposals to retain her as a museum ship, the Admiralty approved *Warspite's* scrapping in July 1946. On 19 April 1947 she departed Portsmouth for the final time, destined for scrapping at Faslane on the River Clyde. On the way she sailed into a severe storm and sank off of Mount's Bay in Cornwall, her skeleton crew rescued by the local Lifeboat Station.

HMS *Warspite* –
Specifications (after 1937 re-fit)

Launched: 26 November 1913

Commissioned: 8 March 1915

Motto: *Belli dura despicio*
(I Despise the Hard Knocks of War)

Once we reached Normandy I slept on the deck and was fed enormous quantities of pasties, or oggies as they were called. As my Action Station was near a 15-inch gun turret the noise was enormous

Midshipman Andrew Hamnett, HMS *Warspite*

74 Operation Deadstick: Pegasus Bridge

There was no doubt that Operation Overlord was a risky operation but out of all the potential hazards, dangers, traps and disasters, there was one aspect that worried the SHAEF planners more than anything else: the Panzers.

The entire left flank of the invasion force was completely unprotected and at the mercy of the enemy's elite Panzer Regiments. The key to protecting this eastern flank of Sword Beach – and with it the entire invasion – were two small bridges that crossed the Caen Canal and the River Orne near the town of Bénouville. With these bridges in Allied hands, the enemy would have to endure a six-hour detour through the centre of Caen to get at the beaches – it was therefore vital that bridges were captured early and captured intact.

The 'honour' of capturing those two bridges would fall to 'D' Company, 2nd (Airborne) Battalion, Oxford and Buckinghamshire Light Infantry under the command of Major John Howard. On 2 May 1944 Howard was given his orders:

Your task is to seize intact the bridges over the River Orne and canal at Bénouville and Ranville, and to hold them until relief...

Operation Deadstick was born.

At 22:56 on 5 June 1944, a Halifax bomber of the RAF took off, towing glider number one. Five others followed suit at one-minute intervals. At 00:07 on 6 June the lead glider passed over the French coast and the formation cut the ties to their bomber escort. They were on their own. In a miraculous feat of flying that Air Chief Marshal Sir Trafford Leigh-Mallory later described as one of the greatest of the entire war, the pilots brought the gliders crashing down on the tiny strip of land separating the two bridges, without alerting the enemy.

Despite being momentarily knocked out from the force of the landing, the passengers of the first glider quickly came to and started to organise themselves for the initial assault. In a matter of minutes, grenades were being dropped into the machine-gun pill-box, clearing out all occupants, and specialist engineers were inspecting the bridge for explosives. The surprise of the attack was a crucial factor; the enemy were caught completely off guard – some were even asleep in the gun pits.

By 00:21 the three glider crews had captured the Bénouville (Pegasus) canal bridge intact and had either killed or chased away practically all German resistance in the vicinity. It had taken just over 10 minutes, but this initial success was not without cost. All three platoon leaders had either been killed or wounded. Meanwhile, over at Ranville, Lieutenant H.J. Sweeny and his platoon took the river bridge without even firing a shot. It was now a case of holding on until the relief arrived. It would be a long wait.

Almost as soon as he had finished his defensive organisations, the sound of enemy armoured vehicles could be heard approaching the west end of the canal bridge. Howard and his men possessed just one PIAT (Projector, Infantry Anti-Tank) launcher with only a couple of rounds. He had to halt the advancing armour, otherwise the bridges would likely be re-taken by the enemy and the success of the entire invasion would be thrown into doubt. Fortunately, the weapon was in the very capable hands of Sergeant Charles Thornton who, waiting until the enemy machine was no more than 20 yards away, made no mistake.

The resulting fireworks display was very impressive indeed, lasting well over an hour and was sufficient to persuade the rest of the German counterattack to fall back. The bridges were safe for the time being, and for his handywork with the PIAT, Sergeant Thornton was awarded the Military Medal.

Pegasus Bridge on 9 June 1944 — a Horsa glider can be seen in the background.

Ham and Jam

As soon as the bridges were captured intact, Major Howard sent out the now famous signal 'Ham and Jam' over the radio. Ham for the canal bridge and Jam for the river bridge

First to be Liberated

British paratroopers entered the Café Gondrée, on the west bank of the Caen canal at 06:20 on D-Day, making it the first building to be liberated by Allied troops

75 The British Airborne assault

The British 6th Airborne Division, commanded by Major General Richard 'Windy' Gale, was dropped between the River Orne and the high ground of the Bois de Bavent to secure the eastern flank of the invasion site.

Like their American paratrooper counterparts, the tasks given to the British Airborne forces mainly involved capturing key crossroads and bridges intact to aid Allied progress inland (such as Pegasus Bridge), neutralising specific enemy strongholds (such as the coastal battery at Merville) and destroying bridges that any German counterattack would need to use, such as those over the River Dives.

At 22:56 on the night of 5 June, six Handley Page Halifax heavy bombers took off from RAF Tarrant Rushton, towing six Horsa gliders – their destination, the bridges over the Caen Canal and the River Orne. A few minutes later another six transports took off, carrying the pathfinders who were to mark out the three drop zones to be used by the rest of the airborne troops. Half an hour later, the first wave of the main airborne assault took to the skies. They were due to be over their drop zones by 00:50 with the second wave arriving at 03:20. A third smaller group, destined for the Merville battery took off last, due to land on top of the stronghold at 04:30. Heavy cloud cover meant that the majority of the pathfinders were dropped

in the wrong place. As a result, much of the the main drop was widely scattered, with some paratroopers landing up to 15 miles off course. The result was a frustrating night for many paratroopers as they struggled to link up with their units. That said, the immediate objectives of capturing the Orne River and Caen Canal bridges, silencing the Merville Battery and destroying the bridges across the River Dives were all carried out successfully.

Although the eastern flank of the invasion was largely secure, there was one gaping hole in the defence line. The village of Bréville was positioned up on a ridge and overlooked the main glider landing zones. While it was still in German hands it presented a huge risk to the security of the Allied bridgehead. At 21:00 on 12 June, after an intense artillery bombardment 'C' Company, 12th Parachute Battalion attacked up the ridge. The Germans reacted quickly and poured very heavy small arms and artillery fire upon the attacking troops. 'C' Company took huge casualties including the Battalion Commander and most of its officers, but they continued to attack. Following closely behind, 'A' Company suffered similarly. It was not until Shermans of the 13th/18th Royal Hussars managed to successfully encircle the village and knock out the enemy positions that things started to quieten down.

Capturing Bréville was vital but costly. 141 of the 160 men that had attacked had either been killed or wounded, but their sacrifice meant that the Germans never attempted a serious attack on the British Airborne Division again.

We saw somebody walking up the sunken road towards us. We asked him for the password and he said, 'Bloody hell, I've forgotten it.' That was our platoon commander

Sergeant Bill French, 7th Battalion, Parachute Regiment

During the initial parachute drop on D-Day, the British 6th Airborne Division suffered

800

casualties

Due to the wide dispersal of the men during the initial drop, it is estimated that no more than 60 per cent of them were able to actively take part in the day's fighting

60%

76 The US Airborne assault

The 101st and 82nd US Airborne Divisions were to be dropped over the western flank of the invasion beaches. The 'Screaming Eagles' of the 101st, were the first to jump. Almost 6,000 men were dropped between 00:48 and 01:40, targeting a drop zone behind Utah Beach. Their first objectives would be to secure the beach exits and move up to the town of Carentan.

An hour later, almost 6,500 men of the 82nd Airborne Division dropped further to the northwest, astride the River Merderet. They were tasked with capturing important bridges on the river and capturing the small but strategically important town of Sainte-Mére-Église, positioned on the main Cherbourg-Bayeux road. Once captured, they were to push as far west as they could.

Even though the operation was well planned, bad weather, a lack of navigators, radio silence and enemy anti-aircraft fire meant that the majority of the men landed far from their drop zones. Some landed in flooded fields, others hit trees and roofs. Most were hopelessly lost and spent the night searching for fellow Americans and trying to avoid enemy patrols.

Much of the 505th Parachute Infantry Regiment of 82nd Airborne Division were dropped over Sainte-Mére-Église with many dropping directly into the laps of the defending German garrison. One soldier landed on the church roof with his parachute tangled around the steeple – he was forced to play dead in an effort to survive. Despite the initial troubles around the landing, Sainte-Mére-Église was secured during the early morning. This was a definite success, but significant pockets of troops were isolated and no contact had been made with the men coming ashore at Utah Beach. In total, by evening, the 82nd Airborne Division had over 1,200 men unaccounted for.

The 101st Airborne also struggled. Only about 2,500 of the original 6,600 men who dropped in Normandy had been accounted for and joined up with fighting units by the evening, but they had seized many of their original objectives, including the exits from Utah Beach and some of the bridges near Carentan.

Paradoxically, the inaccuracy of the drops actually helped to confuse the Germans, whose senior commanders spent the crucial early hours of D-Day trying to make sense of numerous reports of sightings that gave them little indication as to what the Allied plan or strategy was. Like the British drop in the east, the American airborne assault did not go to plan, but it fulfilled its main task.

Airborne Casualties

101st

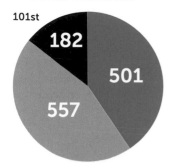

182
501
557

82nd

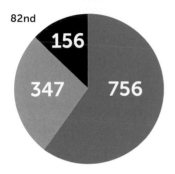

156
347
756

● Killed ● Wounded
● Missing

US National Archives

Moments before the paratroopers of the 101st Airborne Division boarded their aircraft for occupied France, they were visited by General Dwight D. Eisenhower. The paratrooper with the number 23 around his neck is 1st Lieutenant Wallace Strobel.

Dead Man's Corner

Situated to the north of Carentan, the village of Saint-Côme-du-Mont was an important strategic target for the 101st, as it would enable them to launch an attack on Carentan itself. The approaches to Carentan were well covered by the Germans with one of their feared Pak 43 88mm anti-tank gun. The village was dubbed 'Dead Man's Corner' after an Allied tank was hit and destroyed with the commander still sitting upright in the turret

Paratroopers of the 101st Division Airborne on board a C-47 before launch, 6 June 1944

77 Ranville: The first liberation

The first planes to take off as part of Operation Tonga – the British Airborne assault on Normandy – left airbases across the south of England late at the night of 5 June. Flight time was expected to take just 90 minutes and the RAF transports made steady progress. Rousing choruses of 'Onward Christian Soldiers', emanated from several aircraft, but on the whole the noise of the engines made conversation difficult. As the aircraft approached the drop zone and the 20-minute warning rang out, the tension grew and the insides of each plane became consumed with buzz of feverish, focussed activity as the men got ready to jump.

Three of these planes contained three companies of men from the 13th (South Lancashire) Parachute Battalion. They had two objectives: first, to capture and hold Ranville, a small village that guarded the approaches to the Orne bridges from the east, and secondly to clear the obstacles to the north of the village so that gliders could land to bring in reinforcements. 'A' Company was designated to clear obstacles while 'B' and 'C' Companies were tasked to take care of the village.

Hunting horns were used to help the parachutists rendezvous after landing. 'A' Company managed to muster sixty men and, with the help of a team of Royal Engineers armed with explosives, headed off to clear Drop Zone 'N' of any obstacles. The task proved easier than anticipated. The men had been trained to deal with large telegraph poles but many of them were smaller poles, known as 'Rommel's asparagus', and although holes had been dug for the posts, many had simply been placed into the holes, with only a few being properly installed. While 'A' Company and the engineers set about destroying and removing the anti-glider defences, the task of clearing the village of Ranville began.

'C' Company, under Major Gerald Ford, had been ordered to mop up the north end of the village, while Major George Bristow's 'B' Company cleared the southern end. A company of German defenders were at stations in the centre of the village; ironically, however, the majority of them were away on anti-invasion exercises. The machine-gun posts put up minimal resistance and were quickly overrun. There were one or two minor skirmishes in the village with retreating Germans but by 02:30 the village had been cleared and was in British hands.

The liberation of Europe had begun.

Airborne troops beside their Horsa glider, which crashed through a stone wall during its landing on 6th Airborne Division's drop zone near Ranville, 6 June 1944.

First village to be liberated

Ranville was the first village in France to be liberated, by the 13th (South Lancashire) Parachute Battalion at around 02:30 on 6 June 1944

'We quickly worked our way round to the chateau, the Germans having scarpered. I left one Section covering the front of the building, another inside on the ground floor and I went upstairs with Privates Orrel and Prince, where I was met by le Comte de Ranville and his wife, protesting about the intrusion of their property. I tried to tell him that it was the invasion, we were British soldiers and that they were to stay indoors. Back came a torrent of French which I did not understand but they clearly did not believe me. Seeing the key in their bedroom door, I took it out and gave it to them saying in my best 4th Form French, "Lock the door, I'll talk to you in the morning".'

Jack Sharples, 13th (South Lancashire) Parachute Battalion

```
03:00 - Village of RANVILLE
now cleared of enemy. Very
few enemy were found, as
from infm received from
inhabitants, it appears
that the main body of the
enemy were away, and that
the majority of those
left behind departed with
all speed when they saw
parachutists. Those PW taken
were wounded and seemed very
young. Identification from
PW, dead and documents was
7/II Pz Gren Regt 125.
```

WO 171/1246 – excerpt from War Diary (6 June 1944) from 13th (2nd/4th Battalion the South Lancs Regiment) Parachute Battalion.

78 Silencing the Merville Battery

As well as being asked to capture the vital bridges over the Orne, the British 6th Airborne Division had the unenviable task of capturing the mighty Merville Battery, a defensive redoubt which was part of a string of positions in the area designed to protect the important estuary that took maritime traffic directly into Caen.

The Merville Battery was a formidable piece of defensive armour. To defend it from the air were numerous 20 mm anti-aircraft guns and finally there were the big guns – and they were really big – massive 155 mm calibre naval guns that offered up enough firepower to smash the proposed British landing zones some 3 miles away. In light of such danger, it was imperative those guns were silenced before a single Allied foot made it to the beaches.

The task of knocking this monster out of action was given to the 9th Battalion, Parachute Regiment. Leading the assault group was Lieutenant Colonel Terence Otway, and when he hit French soil and discovered that he had landed miles away from the rendezvous point, he was incandescent. As Otway finally arrived at the assembly point, he received three bouts of bad news. First, the planned air strike by the RAF had failed miserably, with not one single bomb hitting the target. Secondly, even worse news followed. His precious glider trains had been lost at sea, meaning he would have to launch the assault without sufficient ammunition,

without jeeps, without mortars, without anti-tank weapons, without lightweight foot-bridges, without machine-guns, without demolition equipment, without medical supplies, without an ambulance and without any real means of communication back to the seaborne army waiting just off the coast for news of success. Finally, it seemed that only 150 men (instead of 750) had made it to the rendezvous point.

Otway had a decision to make. He was woefully short of men and supplies to carry out the job but the guns had to be taken out of action and so, after hastily revising the assault plan, he gave the order to move. It was 02:50 on 6 June 1944.

Each one of Otway's men had a very specific job to do. Well-placed grenades through doors and down ventilation pipes managed to quieten any defenders hiding within the casements, and after twenty minutes of hand-to-hand fighting, the last enemy machine-gun nest fell silent. After knocking out the gun in casement 1, the Germans started to shell the battery in an effort to get rid of the attackers.

Dawn was slowly breaking and Otway became preoccupied with how to get a message back to HMS *Arethusa* before she too started to bombard the battery. The naval gunfire observation party that had dropped with his men had failed to

Number 1 Casemate at the Merville Battery, an historic visitor attraction today.

turn up and the only radio that survived the initial drop was now dead. A yellow flare was found and lit and a pigeon was sent with a message. There was nothing else to do but gather up the wounded and get well away from the battery. Once they had moved out of the area, the Germans reoccupied the battery and although they were able to get two of the guns back working, the battery as a whole was nowhere near as effective as it could be.

The actions of the 9th Battalion had undoubtedly saved many lives on Sword Beach that morning.

Instead of having 750 men to attack the Merville Battery, only

150

made it to the rendezvous position in time for the attack

5 gliders carrying vital equipment for the assault were lost at sea en route to the battery

'The Bangalores went up, there were two enormous explosions, and we ran through shouting and yelling, which is what we always did in training. It did us good and we hoped it frightened the enemy as well. I hadn't got far before something hit my leg and I went down, I was like a sheep on its back, and I watched my men going in and I thought, "My goodness, the training has worked"'

Lt. Alan Jefferson, 9th Battalion, Parachute Regiment

79 Operation Titanic

While the paratroopers were getting themselves ready to drop into France to secure beach exits and neutralise coastal artillery, another group of men were also getting ready for a very different type of action in those first hours of 6 June. The SAS (Special Air Service) was to be engaged in several dangerous but vital deception operations near the landing zones, in an effort to keep German forces away from the beaches.

The suggestion from SHAEF that small groups of lightly armed men, armed only with what they could carry to fend off some of the mightiest armour in the world infuriated SAS leaders – they saw this as nothing more than a suicide mission. In their minds it was ridiculous that scattered groups of parachutists could do anything to deter the arrival of full-strength panzer divisions. They may be able to cause a bit of confusion for a day or two, but without a way of getting fresh supplies their window of effectiveness would be quite small. Feelings ran high and Lieutenant Colonel William Stirling, the Commanding Officer of 2nd SAS Regiment, resigned in protest.

In the final days before the invasion the plans for the SAS teams changed constantly. In the end only a handful of men would be dropped to carry out a plan that was ironically called Operation Titanic.

Operation Titanic was ultimately a series of military deceptions based around a number of simulated parachute drops (using dummies and SAS personnel), carried out as part of the wider Operation Bodyguard cover-up plan intended to confuse German leaders as to the exact details of the planned Allied attack. In total, almost 500 dummy parachutists (known as 'Ruperts') were dropped deep inland behind the invasion beaches.

In addition to all of these dummies, two SAS teams, commanded by Captain Frederick Fowles and Lieutenant Norman Poole were dropped near Saint-Lô. These men carried recordings and amplifiers that played sounds of rifle and mortar fire together with shouted commands. The recordings were played for 30 minutes after landing, before they withdrew from the fake landing zone. If they engaged with Germans, they had orders to ensure some of the enemy escaped so they could spread the word about the large number of parachutists landing in the area.

By 02:00 on 6 June the Germans had reported parachute landings east of Caen and as far west as Saint-Lô. The 7th Army was placed on full invasion alert and Generalfeldmarschall von Rundstedt ordered over half of the 12th SS Panzer Division to deal with an apparent enemy parachute landing near Lisieux, but it was not armed invaders they discovered, just piles of sand, straw and cloth.

The SAS men who landed around Marigny and Saint-Lô managed to divert the German 352nd Infantry Division away from Omaha Beach, Gold Beach and the 101st airborne drop zones. Instead of mounting a counterattack on the beaches, they spent precious hours during the morning of 6 June scouring the woods for parachutists that did not exist.

Overall Operation Titanic achieved its objective, confusing and distracting the German defence forces on the morning of the Allied invasion. Eight members of the SAS never returned; they were either killed during the operation or executed by the Germans at Bergen-Belsen.

Bonhams

Ruperts

The SAS men were accompanied by 500 'Ruperts', crude dummies made of sand, straw and fabric. Each one had a parachute and carried an incendiary device which would fire on landing, removing any evidence that they were not real paratroopers

Trooper Anthony Merryweather

During the operation, Trooper Anthony Merryweather was awarded the Military Medal for gallantry in the field. The citation for the award was raised on the 5 November 1945 by Lieutenant Colonel 'Paddy' Mayne DSO, countersigned by Brigadier J.M. Calvert DSO Commander of the SAS and confirmed by Field Marshal Montgomery.

Trooper Merryweather's MM and SAS badges which were sold at auction on 1 November 2017 for

£14,000

D-Day Normandy Landing Beaches

Valognes

82nd
Airborne
Division

UTAH

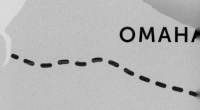

OMAHA

Carentan

N O R M

● Saint Lo

- - - D-Day Objective

10km

GOLD

JUNO

SWORD

Houlgate

Cabourg

Bayeux

Dives

6th Airborne
Division

Caen

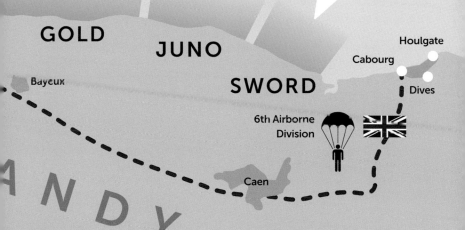

ANDY

80 Utah Beach

Although capturing the deep water port of Cherbourg was viewed as important, the invasion beach codenamed 'Utah' was only added to the Overlord plan in early 1944 and even then it was added through slightly gritted teeth. Landing at Utah was far from ideal – large rivers cut it off from the other landing zones and the low ground immediately inland was routinely flooded by the Germans, which would make any progress inland slow and miserable.

The beach itself was approximately 3 miles long and had four main beach exits which the assaulting troops could use to head inland. The problem was that the Germans knew that the only viable place for a large amphibious landing on this part of the coast was in the north, where low tide was a much more manageable 400 metres and had fortified it accordingly.

In an effort to soften up the enemy before the assault, a huge aerial armada of 9,000 aircraft flew wing-to-wing and smashed the German fortifications defending Utah. This airstrike was backed up by an ongoing naval bombardment aimed at the beaches themselves. It was an awe-inspiring sight that gave the men of the 4th US Infantry Division, who were waiting offshore, a feeling of hope that they could take the beach.

The initial plan was to land floating Duplex Drive (DD) tanks first at about 06:30. There would be thirty-two of these tanks, carried forward by eight LCTs (Landing Craft, Tanks). Right behind them would be twenty LCAs (Landing Craft, Assault, better known as Higgins boats) each carrying a thirty-man assault team from the 2nd Battalion, 8th US Infantry Regiment. A second wave of thirty-two LCAs carrying men from the 1st Battalion (plus engineers and demolition teams) would come in five minutes later. Wave three carried in more amour, including Sherman and bulldozer tanks, and was planned for H plus fifteen minutes. A fourth wave would follow a couple of minutes later.

Brigadier General Theodore Roosevelt Jr, son of the former president and cousin of the current one, had led his men ashore during the first wave of the assault. He now had a decision to make. Should he attempt to move his entire landing force more than a mile up the coast and attempt to land in the correct place, following the original plan, or should he continue the landings at the current position? It did not take him long to make up his mind and he allegedly said, 'We'll start the war from right here.'

By the time the second wave approached the beach the Germans had finally woken up and started to hit the landing zones with 88 mm shells, mortars and machine-gun fire. Despite being under constant fire all day, Roosevelt repeatedly led his men up to and over the seawall and pointed them the way inland.

His leadership, decisiveness and bravery on the beach that morning won him the Congressional Medal of Honor and also went a long way to ensuring the beach was secured within just three hours of the initial landings.

The Utah landings were one of the major successes of the D-Day operations.

In fifteen hours more than 20,000 men and 1,700 vehicles of various size and shape landed on Utah Beach. Casualties for the US 4th Infantry Division were 197, with approximately 700 additional losses from engineering units, LCTs and other vessels sunk by the enemy.

US National Archives

Scene on Utah Beach, with troops marching up the road, 9 June 1944. Note rolled wooden slats (used to stabilise beach roadway) among the items in the foreground.

As the men waited offshore for H-Hour,

9,000

Allied aircraft bombarded the German defences around Utah

By the end of the day

23,250

and 1,742 vehicles were ashore on Utah. The US 4th Infantry Division suffered

197 casualties

'I jumped out in waist deep water, we had 200 feet to go to shore and you couldn't run, you could just kind of push forward. We finally made it to the edge of the water, then we had 200 yards of open beach to cross, through the obstacles. But fortunately, most of the Germans were not able to fight, they were all shook up from the bombing and the shelling and the rockets and most of them just wanted to surrender'

Sergeant Malvin Pike, E Company,
2nd Battalion, 8th Infantry Regiment,
US 4th Division

US 4th Infantry
vanguard

81 Omaha Beach

Two-thirds of all American resource and effort on D-Day was concentrated on the landing zone known by the codename 'Omaha'. It was a pivotal sector of the invasion front, as this was where the bulk of the American men and resource would be landing in an effort to link up with the vital flanks of Caen in the east and the port of Cherbourg in the west.

The gently sloping sand and shingle beach was 5,000 yards long and dominated by large sandy 'bluffs' (mini cliffs that rose up over 30 metres) that created a massive natural barrier and limited the available routes on and off the beach. Due to the slight concave curve to the coastline, these bluffs had a complete and dominant view over the entire landing zone. If this was not enough, strong offshore currents created sand banks and small valleys under the water that were exposed at low tide and created huge issues for any landing craft and vehicles trying to get ashore.

In January 1944, Captain Scott-Bowden of the Special Boat Service undertook a detailed reconnaissance of the Omaha landing zone. When reporting back to General Omar Bradley he commented that he believed the beach contained the most formidable natural defence system of the entire front which would

unquestionably result in large numbers of casualties.

The Germans had long since recognised the potential of this long and open stretch of beach as a likely invasion zone and had planned their regional coastal defences accordingly. Everything Rommel had learned during World War 1 about stopping a full-on frontal assault was put into practice at Omaha. Thousands upon thousands of iron structures, wooden poles and jagged steel 'hedgehogs' – many decorated with anti-tank mines or modified artillery shells – were planted up and down the beach from the low-tide mark to the high-tide point, forming an almost impenetrable, and very explosive, defensive shield in front of the beach.

The approach to the beaches would be a nightmare, and that was before any man even set foot on terra firma.

If the attacking troops managed to weave a path through all of that, they faced a long journey over an open beach that was completely overlooked by steep bluffs brimming with firepower that would enjoy a clear and uninterrupted view of the entire beach, especially the five exits cut into the bluffs themselves. Rommel singled out these exits for special treatment. Not only were they overlooked by numerous strongpoints but each one was further reinforced with large concrete roadblocks, even more wire, numerous booby-traps and thousands of mines.

The overall strength of defensive power on Omaha was frightening: there were eight large concrete bunkers each containing heavy 88 mm or 75 mm guns, another sixty light artillery guns, thirty-five smaller artillery positions, eighteen anti-tank guns, eighty-five machine-gun nests and one central strongpoint housing flamethrowers. Running between all of these strongpoints and gun positions were miles of trenches concealing almost one hundred machine-guns. Furthermore, set back on top of the bluffs were numerous rocket launchers and mortar positions, ready and primed to blast the beaches to pieces. Last, but definitely not least, were the massive 155 mm guns of the Maisy Battery, positioned on the western end of Omaha on top of a 100-foot cliff called Pointe du Hoc. Both Omaha and Utah beaches were within range of these monsters. There was not one single inch of Omaha Beach that was not under direct fire from a multitude of weapons.

The task of landing on Omaha was handed to the men of the US 116th Regiment and the US 16th Infantry Regiment. Their plan of attack was intricate and precise. H-Hour was set for 06:30 and as the first assault wave prepared for their journey to the beach, the men bobbing up and down in their LCAs (Landing Craft, Assault) heard wave upon wave of Allied heavy bombers heading inland to smash the beach to bits. Note that they only heard them. They did not see them due to low-lying cloud. Unfortunately, just as much as the men could not see the bombers, the bombers could not see their targets. They had to drop their bombs 'blind'. The crews were desperately trying to avoid bombing their own men and subsequently delayed the release of the bombs by a few seconds. As a result, the vast majority of the 13,000 Allied bombs that were dropped fell harmlessly inland.

At H minus 40 minutes the battleships USS *Texas* and USS *Arkansas* launched an awe-inspiring bombardment on to the enemy strongpoints, but again due to low cloud it was very difficult to ascertain accuracy of fire and much of this naval fire missed its intended target.

The infantry attack would see the US 116th Regiment and the US 16th Regiment advancing side by side. The first wave would consist of two battalions of each regiment as well as DD tanks, navy underwater demolition teams and army engineers. The demolition teams were tasked with blowing a path through the substantial underwater obstacle course, marking the safe path with flags so subsequent waves of landing craft would know where to safely drop off their fighting cargo. The frogmen had 30 minutes to complete this task before the second wave of landing craft was scheduled to arrive. After which, new assault teams, along with huge numbers of battle equipment such as tanks, jeeps, communication units, medical equipment, big guns, trucks, etc., would arrive at the beach every 10 minutes until 09:30. By H-Hour plus 120 minutes it was expected that the invasion force would be driving out of the beach exits on their journey inland towards their D-Day objectives.

US National Archives

Medics treat injured soldiers on Omaha Beach.

That was the plan, but before a single boot had set foot on Omaha Beach that plan was disintegrating. The air and naval bombardments had failed. As the ramps on the boats were lowered all hell was let loose. In an instant, Omaha Beach was transformed into a blazing inferno. Machine-gun fire slaughtered the men coming down the ramps. 'A' Company of the 116th US Infantry lost 96 per cent of its effective fighting strength before any of them had fired a shot.

In a last throw of the dice, a number of naval destroyers, including the USS *Texas*, were manoeuvred as close to the shore as was physically possible and they started to blast the bluffs at what was effectively point-blank range. Slowly but surely, with the help of Allied air force spotters directing fire, the German strong points were silenced one by one.

By 21:00 the planned infantry landings for D-Day was completed. 34,000 men had managed to get ashore, but not without heavy losses of men and materials.

741st Tank Battalion

The 741st Tank Battalion (TB) supported the 16th Infantry Regiment with armour. All sixteen tanks from 'C' Company sank on the way to the beach, as did thirteen of the sixteen tanks from 'B' Company. During the day, only five amphibious DD tanks, six tanks equipped with snorkels and five bulldozer tanks manage to reach the shore. By the end of the day only three tanks were still operational

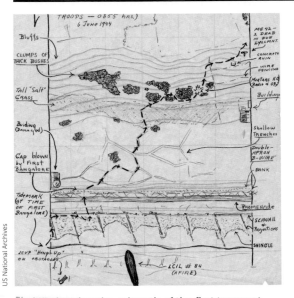

Sketch showing the exit path of the first troops at 08:55 hours in the 'Dog White' sector of Omaha Beach on D-Day.

The maximum depth of the push inland from Omaha was just **1.5** miles

Omaha was the bloodiest of the invasion beaches. Accurate numbers are not known but estimates suggest the numbers of killed, missing and wounded were between

2,000
and
5,000

In contrast, the German 352nd division suffered approximately

1,200

killed, wounded and missing – about 20% of its strength

82 The German defence of Omaha

Over the years, the Normandy Landings have largely been discussed from an Allied perspective, with very little time or effort given to understanding what it must have been like for the soldiers and men of the German Wehrmacht who occupied the Atlantic Wall defences overlooking the beaches.

One such soldier was Obergefreiter Heinrich Severloh, a veteran of the Eastern Front who, on D-Day, found himself paired with a heavy machine-gun within the strongpoint Widerstandsnest (resistance nest) 62 or WN62 – one of the forward defence strongpoints that overlooked Omaha Beach.

Severloh wrote about his experiences of D-Day in a book called WN62. Below is an extract which describes the moment the first wave of US infantry approached Omaha Beach in the early morning of 6 June 1944.

At shortly before 0630, after the heavy salvos of the battleships had stopped, I noticed a large, thin and tall boat in our bay, coming from the northeast toward our wide, ebb-tide beach directly in front of our sector, and 600 metres from Strongpoint WN62. It was a troop landing ship with a shallow hull and a pointed bow, on either side of which large gang-planks were lowered. A large number of soldiers appeared at the railing, and began to go down the gangplanks, loaded down with weapons and equipment.

One could see it quite clearly. Though we had always spoken of the 'Tommies' we expected, I could see immediately from the shape of the helmets and the large, white letters US, on the bow of the transport that they were Americans. They descended the gangplanks calmly, in orderly columns, and jumped into the cold, chest-to-shoulder-high water. Many went under for a moment and, half swimming, half wading, they began to move slowly toward the beach in front of our strongpoint.

At this time, it was almost completely quiet in the bay, and not a single shot was being fired. We had strict orders to wait until the GIs were only about 400 metres from the upper beach, and in knee-deep water. I ran to the communications bunker about twenty metres distant, and called:

'Now it's starting; they're landing!'

The operators, who were constantly busy with the telephone and radio, couldn't leave their bunker, and for that reason they couldn't know what was going on outside. One of them said to me, 'Hein, when you can, let us know what is going on down there on the beach...'

Then, I ran back through the trench the few steps to my machine-gun. By that time, more and more soldiers had disembarked from the transport. After the Americans got a footing they waded in two long columns, one behind the other, through the water, and each held on to the belt of the one in front with his left hand. Everything went in such a cool and orderly way, as if they were merely conducting a training exercise.

Lieutenant Frerking appeared next to me in the trench, and we observed how the Americans, loaded down with weapons and equipment, toiled slowly forward, completely defenceless, through the high swells of the cold salt water. It was to us that the GI's down there were about to enter into their own slaughterhouse. 'Poor swine...' Frerking said softly to himself; then he went down into the bunker to give the co-ordinates and firing order for the artillery. As I turned back to my machine-gun position, I also had the feeling that I was ascending the scaffold...

It had lasted about five minutes until the Americans reached the shallow water. I noticed then, for the first time that day, that there were soldiers of the Grenadier Regiment 726 at our strongpoint for, somewhat further down beneath my machine-gun position, a sergeant and another infantryman were trying frantically to get a machine-gun into action – but it wasn't working.

I'm not the type to look for trouble; I hadn't thought of any such thing: whatever for? Behind me, the entrance to the strongpoint was mined and barricaded with a thick barrier of barbed wire. Anyway, I was a soldier; a soldier who was going to be attacked, and as such I now had to defend myself. I moved the safety lock of my machine-gun to the off position and began to fire. I could see the water spouts where my machine-gun bursts were hitting, and when the little fountains got close to the GI's they threw themselves down. After only a few seconds, panic broke out among the Americans. They all lay in the shallow, cold water; many tried to get to the most forward beach obstacle to find some cover behind them. Soon the first corpses drifted about in the waves of the slowly rising tide. I fired further among the many dark forms in the water, which were still about 300 metres from the upper beach. After a little while, all the GI's on the beach had been brought down. Suddenly, I had the impression that mine was the only gun in our entire sector that had fired. It is true that my machine-gun made so much noise that I could hardly have heard the others; nevertheless, it seemed to me that I actually had fired completely alone, as I only observed the panicky reaction of the Americans at those places in the water where I had aimed....

Excerpt taken from *WN62: A German Soldier's Memories of the Defence of Omaha Beach, Normandy, June 6, 1944.* English version published in 2011 by HEK Creativ Verlag, Garbsen, Germany.

83 Pointe Du Hoc

About 5 miles to the west of Omaha, a commanding piece of the coastline projected out to sea. The French called it La Pointe du Hoc; in reality it was nothing more than a 100-foot-high cliff, but on D-Day this little piece of cliff was as strategically important to the Americans as Pegasus Bridge and the Merville Battery were to the British.

There were six reasons why the Americans poured so much attention and scrutiny on to this little patch of French coastline: six 155 mm naval cannons stolen from the French, that were perched high on top of this particular cliff, each with a range of 12 miles. Allied bombers had been smashing the area as best they could since May, dropping more than 10,000 tonnes of high explosives, but there was no guarantee that the guns were out of action – they would need to be taken out manually.

Due to the position of the guns it would be difficult to use an airborne assault. Somehow, these guns would have to be attacked directly from the sea. In effect, this meant after getting ashore, men would have to scale the cliff under the noses of the enemy to get to the guns. On paper it looked difficult; in reality, when you factored in the enemy peering over the edge, cutting ropes and throwing bombs and grenades at the invader, it looked practically impossible and would need a very special group of men to even attempt such an attack.

Enter the 2nd Battalion, US Rangers.

Led by Colonel James E. Rudder, the US Rangers were some of the finest fighting men America had to offer. They had been training for this day in Scotland with the British Royal Marine Commandos for a very long time, practising coastal assaults against cliffs.

The plan was for three companies to assault the guns directly from the sea – a total force of just 255 men. They were to land at 06:30, after a naval barrage from USS *Texas*, which would smash the cliffs for 35 minutes. Another Ranger company – 'C' company – was to land on the far right-hand edge of Omaha Beach, move quickly inland and follow the heavily fortified coastal road to join up with the rest of the Rangers at the gun position. Another two companies were held back in reserve, due to land at Pointe du Hoc at 07:30.

That was the plan. However, just as with the main landings at Omaha, the plan had to be abandoned even before a shot had been fired.

At H minus forty minutes USS *Texas* opened fire at cliff and the gun positions, lifting her fire as scheduled, 5 minutes before the first assault craft were due to land on the beach. The problem was, those first LCAs were heading in the wrong direction. In the pre-dawn light, a combination of navigational error and a strong current pushed the LCAs too far east and they were actually moving towards the Pointe Percée. By the time the error had been spotted and the boats turned around, a DUKW and an LCA had been lost to enemy fire. The Rangers were down to 180 men before they even landed on the beach.

Of the sixty-eight Rangers from 'C' Company who landed first, only thirty-one made it to the base of the cliff. USS *Satterlee* and HMS *Talybont* drew in as close to the coast line as they could and fired on the cliffs with everything they had – a group of B-26 bombers joined in from the air and between them forced the German defenders on top of the cliff to take cover, giving the Rangers a small window of opportunity to scale the cliffs. By 07:45 all surviving Rangers were on top of the cliff and involved in a fearsome firefight with the enemy. Eventually, the enemy was subdued enough for the Rangers to turn their attention to the gun emplacements. The guns were not there.

In their place were telephone poles. A patrol was sent out immediately to find them and by 09:00 they had been discovered, set up and ready to fire in an orchard about 200 yards inland. The guns were quickly destroyed with a couple of well-placed thermite grenades. They were eventually relieved on 8 June. Of the 225 Rangers who landed on D-Day, 135 had become casualties.

US National Archives

US Army Rangers with ladders used to storm the cliffs at Pointe du Hoc.

French civilians executed

The Rangers accused several French civilians of fighting alongside the enemy, shooting at American forces or of serving as artillery observers for the Germans. A number of French locals were executed on such grounds

84 Gold Beach

Gold Beach was smack in the middle of the five designated landing zones for the Allied invasion. It was 5 miles wide and took in the coast towns of La Rivière and Le Hamel as well as the small port of Arromanches. Gold was the most westerly of the British landing zones and butted up right against Omaha. The beach itself was mostly flat and rose gently inland. In places the beach was desperately shallow, leading right up to the Atlantic Wall. The Germans had fortified this area strongly; the beach was heavily sown with almost 2,500 obstacles and mines of various sizes and shapes. There were miles of barbed wire strung around any potential exit routes, with yet more mines and booby-traps hidden to surprise any potential invader. Beach-side houses were turned into machine-gun strongpoints and snipers' nests, all arranged meticulously to give the defenders the best field of fire possible.

Then there were the big guns.

In late 1943 and early 1944 the cliffs at Les Longues situated between the Omaha and Gold beaches were a hive of construction activity as a monumental coastal battery was built to defend the coastline. When completed it boasted four 5.9-inch naval guns taken directly from decommissioned naval destroyers. They had an effective range of 12 miles and could fire directly upon Omaha, Gold and Juno beaches.

As well as the four monster naval guns, there were six machine-gun pits and a mortar pit, and an anti-aircraft gun provided some extra fire-power and protection. The clever people at SHAEF had obviously recognised the threat of the battery and in pre-invasion bombardments in late May and early June 1944 bomber formations dropped 150 tonnes of explosives directly on to the gun casements. Unfortunately, they did not even make a dent.

The task of capturing Gold Beach was handed to the British 50th Infantry Division. Facing them were a mixture of Russian conscripts and highly trained German soldiers, many of whom were positioned in houses along the coast which did not offer the best protection from air and sea bombardments.

H-Hour was set for 07:25 – an hour behind the Americans – with a naval bombardment commencing at 03:00. Within 20 minutes HMS *Ajax* had fired 114 shells and had succeeded in silencing the dangerous Les Longues battery. Coastal defences were smashed and because many of the German defenders had taken up positions in beach-side houses, a large number were completely destroyed.

Seven minutes later the first assault troops hit the beach. In that first wave were men from the 1st Battalion Royal Hampshire Regiment. As soon as the ramps went down in those leading landing craft, they started to take serious casualties. The Battalion's Commanding Officer and his second-in-command were killed within minutes from machine-gun fire. In those first critical moments the situation on Gold was so bad it looked like a mirror image of what was going on at Omaha.

The 1st Hampshire's continued to encounter fierce opposition and they were not able to capture the seaside village of Le Hamel until mid-afternoon. On the Hampshire's left flank, the 6th Battalion, Green Howards and the 1st Battalion, Dorset Regiment landed under less intense enemy fire and within an hour or so they had consolidated their sector and were on the way inland, marching behind flail tanks that were proving very adept at clearing a safe path through the various mine-fields.

Company Sergeant Major Stan Hollis of the Green Howards was the only British soldier to win the Victoria Cross during the fighting on D-Day

'The beach was strewn with wreckage, a blazing tank, bundles of blankets and kit, bodies and bits of bodies....'

Gunner Charles Wilson, 147th (Essex Yeomanry) Field Regiment, Royal Artillery

24,970

men landed on Gold Beach during D-Day, along with

2,100

vehicles and one thousand tons of supplies

US National Archives

The British had established a beachhead 6 miles wide by 6 miles deep and managed to link up with the Canadians on their left. All for the loss of only 400 casualties. It was a truly remarkable achievement.

85 Sword Beach

In the eyes of Montgomery, the landing zones on Sword Beach were key. They were also some of the most dangerous.

Key, because a successful landing on Sword, the most easterly of the invasion beaches, would put the Allies within striking distance of the strategically vital city of Caen. Not only was Caen an important communications hub, its capture would also significantly slow down any planned counterattack from the Pas-de-Calais region – an area teeming with panzer regiments that could cause the Allies no end of trouble if they got too close.

This imminent threat of a counterattack made Sword Beach the most vulnerable landing zone. The beach was closest to the enemy and would most likely bear the brunt of any major enemy counterattack. It was also well within range of the huge Merville Battery and other large in-land batteries code-named 'Morris' and 'Hillman', each of which possessed more than enough fire power to smash the beach to pieces.

The task fell to the British 3rd Division to land on a very narrow front of just one brigade. Once ashore they were to make a beeline for Caen. Their orders were explicit: by nightfall they were to have 'captured or effectively masked' the city. Once this had been completed, they were to link up with the British 6th Airborne Division who would be holding on to the

vital bridges over the Orne waterways. All of this had to be completed whilst avoiding the 21st Panzer Division, which was known to be in the area and within striking distance.

At 05:45 an impressive naval fleet of two battleships, five cruisers and thirteen destroyers opened up a ferocious bombardment on to the beach defences as well as a number of the inland batteries. H-Hour was set for 07:25.

The DD Tanks were scheduled to be first ashore, however, as on the other invasion beaches, they struggled in the high tides and strong currents and a number of LCTs and LCAs overtook them. By 07:26 the first landing craft were hitting the beach. They were greeted by enemy machine-gun and mortar fire, not as bad as Omaha or Juno but still significant. In those first decisive minutes, casualties were heavy.

Immediately behind the first wave came the first section of LCTs carrying Sherman Tanks and a multitude of Hobart's Funnies that immediately got to work clearing mines, breaking through barbed-wire entanglements and bridging anti-tank ditches. Enemy fire from a number of isolated strongpoints continued to cause heavy casualties until a machine-gun platoon of the 2nd Middlesex Regiment landed and immediately got into the action with their heavy Vickers guns. Within an hour or so most of the beach was secure; however, in the area around Lion-sur-Mer the enemy continued to mount a stubborn resistance.

At 08:20 No. 4 Commando landed on the beach opposite Lion-sur-Mer. Its target was to get to the Orne Bridges and meet up with the 6th Airborne. When the ramps went down, they took immediate casualties. With the help of a number of DD Tanks the Commandos slowly pushed the enemy back, split into two groups and by noon Ouistreham was liberated. By the end of the day the British had fallen just short of their original objective of taking the city of Caen, a mistake that would turn out to be costly in the coming days and weeks. However, they had managed to get almost 29,000 men ashore with less than 700 casualties (killed, missing or wounded), had repelled an enemy counterattack and had secured the eastern flank of the invasion beachhead.

Shakespeare on Sword

As the first assault wave approached the beach Major C.K. King DSO tried to inspire the men of 'A' Company, 2nd East Yorkshire Regiment by reading extracts of Shakespeare's *King Henry V* over his craft's Tannoy system

East Yorkshire Regiment landing on Queen Red Sector, Sword Beach.

28,845 men

and 223 tanks

came ashore on Sword Beach on D-Day

There were approximately **630** casualties

Bullets just came at you like raindrops. You could hear them whistling and pass you and hitting the ground near you but you just kept going on

Private William Edward Lloyd, 2nd Battalion, East Yorkshire Regiment

86 Juno Beach

To the east of Gold Beach was the beach codenamed 'Juno', and it was here where men of the 3rd Canadian Division, under the command of Major General Rod Keller, would try and get ashore on D-Day. Many of the men approaching the beach just before dawn on 6 June had already seen action in France – they had been involved in the disastrous 1942 Dieppe Raid that resulted in 3,623 Canadians dead, missing or wounded. The 2,400 men that made up the first wave of attackers were determined this would not be a repeat performance.

The 6-mile stretch of coastline that became known as Juno ran between Courseulles-sur-Mer and Saint-Aubin-sur-Mer, and was sandwiched between the two British beaches – Sword and Gold. Compared to other areas, this particular stretch of the Normandy coastline was not heavily fortified. The Kriegsmarine (the Germany navy) was convinced that a heavy defensive network was not worthwhile, predominately because of the large offshore rocks, exposed at low tide, that protected the approach to the beach area.

The night before the invasion, the RAF led numerous bombing raids on the Juno defences but unfortunately very few bombs landed on their designated targets. At first light the USAAF took over but a combination of poor visibility and a fear of dropping their bombs on to the attacking troops meant they delayed

their drop for a few vital seconds. Consequently, the majority dropped harmlessly inland. It was followed by the naval bombardment which started at 06:00 and looked impressive enough. However, such massive firepower threw up so much smoke and debris that it was impossible to see if it was working or not. The bombardment finished at 07:30, 5 minutes before the first wave was due to hit the beach, but because of the threat of the off-shore rocks, it was decided to wait 20 minutes to give the approaching landing craft a bit more water clearance. These extra 20 minutes may have made it easier to get ashore, but it also gave the German defenders time to dust themselves down and get back to their guns.

As the first ramps went down on the leading landing craft, enemy fire was conspicuous by its absence. It was very quiet. Perhaps the naval guns had done their job and smashed the defences to pieces? Maybe the enemy had all been killed or had fled inland? Sadly, neither situation was true. The enemy was there and ready, with their guns trained on the beach rather than the sea, and as soon as the Canadians started to wade ashore, they were hit by intense machine-gun and artillery fire.

Without cover from tanks, which were delayed due to rough seas, that first wave of attackers had only a 50/50 chance of survival. During those first vital minutes it was touch and go as to whether the landings on Juno would succeed. It was not until the DD Tanks and other armoured brigades eventually started to arrive on the beach that some of the gun positions were silenced. Then, in the midst of the battle, with machine-gun bullets and shrapnel flying, the pipers of the Canadian Scottish Regiment started to play. They had played when the Regiment had set sail from England, they had played as they boarded their landing craft and nothing was going to stop them playing their pipes on the beach.

Within an hour a safe path through the minefield had been created and identified with white tape, and after just two hours Juno Beach was secured. It was time to push inland. By the end of the day the Canadians had firmly established a deep beachhead, reaching the villages of Anisy and Mathieu – some 7 miles inland.

21,400
men and
3,200
vehicles landed on Juno Beach during D-Day

Canadian soldiers stream on to Juno Beach.

Library and Archives Canada

'The German machine-gunners in the dunes were absolutely stupefied to see a tank emerge from the sea. Some ran away, some just stood up in their nests and stared, mouths wide open. To see tanks coming out of the water shook them rigid'

Sergeant Léo Gariépy, Canadian 6th Armoured Regiment

Juno beach was divided into three landing zones – from west to east. They were...

340
soldiers killed

574
soldiers wounded

47
taken prisoner

87 Sainte-Mère-Église

Sainte-Mère-Église is 7 miles inland from Utah Beach, situated roughly halfway between Montebourg and Carentan and was at the centre of a network of roads that ran in and out of the town like a spider's web. It was this proximity to both the landing zones and a large number of important roads, that caught the eye of the D-Day planners. If they could drop an airborne division or two into the area around Sainte-Mère-Église, they stood a good chance of preventing local German reinforcements slamming into the troops coming ashore at Utah.

Control Sainte-Mère-Église and you control the area.

On D-Day it was the task of the American 82nd Airborne Division to secure Sainte-Mère-Église, as well as securing several bridges over the Merderet River. As the men prepared for their drop a house in the town square had caught fire, possibly from marker flares or a stray incendiary. As a result, the townspeople and the entire German garrison were wide awake trying to put out the fire. The locals had formed a chain with buckets from the pump in the town square in an effort to quell the flames. It was at about this time when the first parachutes were spotted from the ground.

Men from the 101st and 82nd Airborne Divisions were coming down in the vicinity of the town. Most of the parachutists landed safely in the dark

fields around Sainte-Mère-Église, but some of them – primarily from 'F' Company, 505th Parachute Infantry Regiment 82nd Airborne Division – were coming down in the very centre of the town, where the light from the burning house made it easy for the Germans to spot them. Many paratroopers were shot before they had even hit the ground.

Lieutenant Colonel Benjamin Vandervoort of the 505th Parachute Infantry Regiment had the primary objective of securing the town of Sainte-Mère-Église. Breaking his ankle on landing, he corralled a number of men from the 101st Airborne Division that had dropped miles from their objective to commandeer a cart and pull him towards the town, oblivious to the chaos in the town square.

Meanwhile, on the outskirts of the town Lieutenant Colonel Edward Krause had gathered over one hundred men and was preparing to enter the town. He instructed the men to use only knives and grenades if they encountered the enemy, as that way they would be able to identify any muzzle flashes as being that of the enemy, thus pinpointing their location.

To Krause's surprise the majority of the German garrison had largely fled after the initial skirmish in the town square, leaving behind just a handful of snipers. These were quickly dealt with and by

17:30 the town of Sainte-Mère-Église had been liberated.

As dawn broke, Lieutenant Colonel Vandervoort arrived in the town on a makeshift two-wheel stretcher along with several hundred men he had managed to pick up along the way. They were unaware that the town was already in American hands and more confusion reigned as they started the process of 'clearing' individual houses. Once the situation became clear, Vandervoort's men moved out to the north of the town and set up defensive positions along the main Cherbourg Road.

Museums and monuments

The building that was set on fire in the middle of Sainte-Mère-Église is now a museum for the 82nd Airborne Division and the water pump used by civilians is now a protected monument

'The first thing I remember seeing as I descended was a large spire in a bunch of buildings that later proved to be Sainte-Mère-Église. I started receiving very heavy light flak and machine-gun fire from the ground. This was absolutely terrifying'

Spencer Wurst, 505th Parachute Infantry Regiment, 82nd Airborne Division

Private John Steele

Private John Steele of 'F' Company 505th PIR 82nd Airborne Division jumped into Normandy on the night of 5/6 June 1944. Poor weather conditions led to a scattered drop and thirty-six men of Steele's company came down into the church square of Sainte-Mère-Église where they were captured or killed. Some buildings in the village were on fire, which illuminated the night sky, making easy targets of the descending paratroopers. Steele's parachute caught on the church tower where he hung for two hours feigning death. He was eventually taken prisoner for a further two hours before he escaped and rejoined his unit. Steele was awarded the Bronze Star and Purple Heart for his exploits in Normandy. His experience was famously recreated by the actor Red Buttons in the film *The Longest Day*

88 Villers-Bocage

In the wake of the D-Day landings on 6 June 1944, the Allies had made rapid progress inland in what became the Battle of Normandy and by 12th June Allied formations had reached the outskirts of the strategically important port city of Caen.

Central to the Allied plan was to take control of the main trunk road towards Caen, and the high ground overlooking the road, known as Hill 213. To do this they would also have to take control of a small town by the name of Villers-Bocage. Under the command of Brigadier William 'Loony' Hinde, British spearheads had reached the outskirts of the town by the morning of 13 June.

Meanwhile, Waffen-SS divisional comm-ander SS-Obergruppenführer Josef 'Sepp' Dietrich had anticipated this move by the British and had instructed SS-Obersturmführer Michael Wittmann and his small squad of Tigers to make their way to the area. Wittmann arrived on 12 July and took up a position south of Hill 213 on the Villers-Bocage ridge close to the Vire-Caen road in support of both the Panzer-Lehr and the 12th Hitlerjugend Panzer Divisions.

The British column pressed on towards Hill 213, completely unaware that the enemy were also active in the area. On reaching the high ground, which gave them an uninterrupted view down towards Caen, the column stopped to allow the men to stretch their legs and have a cup of tea.

The kettle had hardly finished boiling when Michael Wittmann's Tiger Tank emerged from cover and started to charge towards the rear of the column. After knocking out the rear tank he continued to drive down the road, shooting up and destroying subsequent vehicles. The crews all fled, leaving their vehicles at the mercy of the rampant Tiger.

At 10:00, the tank company positioned on Hill 213 reported being surrounded and attacked by Tiger Tanks. Half an hour later, Lieutenant Colonel Viscount Cranley reported that his position was untenable and withdrawal impossible. At 10:35 all contact with the British tanks on Point 213 was lost.

At 12:40, Viscount Cranley – somewhere on Hill 213 but out of touch with his tanks – radioed for a second time that he was surrounded; and at about 13:00 the surviving British armour on Hill 213 surrendered. Cranley was captured separately and taken prisoner.

Sometime after 13:00, SS-Haupt-sturmführer Rolf Möbius ordered his 1st Company Tigers to advance into Villers-Bocage, but after losing three tanks to close-range weapons, they withdrew, allowing the British to move into place covering the main approaches to the town. By 16:00 enemy infantry were reported in the southeast corner of Villers-Bocage and within an hour a British withdrawal was sanctioned, despite having 131 Brigade, complete with full tank battalion, two infantry battalions, and an artillery regiment sitting ready to go, just a couple of miles away.

By 20:00, just twelve hours after the British had wistfully entered Villers-Bocage to the sounds of cheering from residents, the Germans had complete control of the town, with the British forced to defend a tenuous position on high ground to the west.

The leading battle group of the 22nd British Armoured Brigade had been destroyed, recording the loss of 217 men (killed, wounded, missing or taken prisoner), twenty-seven tanks (and thirty armoured transport vehicles). On the German side, twenty-three men were lost (killed, missing or wounded) and six Tiger Tanks were destroyed, along with two Panzer IV tanks.

Unused resources

According to the 22 Brigade War Diary, at 21:30 on 13 June, after the withdrawal from Villers-Bocage, the brigade still had

155
tanks operational, well over one hundred of which had not fired a shot all day

'(The Tiger) immediately knocked out Colonel Arthur's tank, and that of the regimental second in command, Major Carr, who he seriously wounded, followed by the Regimental Sergeant Major's tank. Captain Dyas in the fourth tank, reversed and backed into the front garden of a nearby house'

Major W.H.J. Sale,
4 County of London
Yeomanry

WikiCommons

Knocked-out Cromwell tank, commanded by Captain Paddy Victory of 5th Royal Horse Artillery, 7th Armoured Division, in Villers-Bocage

89 Operation Epsom

Operation Epsom, also known as the Battle of Odon was the first major offensive launched by the British after the D-Day landings. Epsom had two objectives. Firstly, to draw the bulk of the German armour in the area on to the British and Canadians, thus preventing Rommel from moving any of his panzer divisions west towards the American front. Secondly, Montgomery was desperate to take the town of Caen – one of the original objectives of D-Day – as it would give his Second Army a platform from which to push further south towards Falaise and beyond.

The offensive was to be carried out by the 11th Armoured, 15th (Scottish) and 43rd (Wessex) Divisions and was originally pencilled in for 18 June, however a large storm hit the area at that time and for three days the Allies were only able to land a fraction of the men and supplies they needed for the offensive. This delay was crucial, as during this time the mighty 2nd SS Panzer Corps had reached Normandy.

On 25 June the 49th (West Riding) Division, fighting its first ever battle, moved forward in thick mist against stiff German opposition. Although they made some progress, they failed to get as far as Raury, meaning that the right-hand side flank of the offensive was in German hands.

The poor weather continued and heavy rain during the night of 25/26 June meant that the planned preliminary air bombardment had to be cancelled. Montgomery did not want to postpone the attack again, so early on the morning of 26 June 500 artillery guns barked into life to commence a three-hour long bombardment, supported by a fleet of naval guns anchored off the Normandy coast. Despite the impressive show, the barrage did little to dent the German defensive lines. By the end of the day progress had been disappointingly slow. The 15th (Scottish) Division had not even got halfway to the Odon.

However, the Germans were panicking. Rommel cancelled a planned offensive of his own to release reinforcements to prop up the line and the next day he threw seventy tanks into a counter-attack, but they were quickly dispelled by cleverly positioned anti-tank defences, and by the end of the day the 15th (Scottish) Division had captured a bridge over the Oden and by the morning of 28 June the tanks of the 11th Armoured Division had crossed the river.

Later that day the British managed to capture the slopes of Hill 112 but were unable to secure the summit. Allied reconnaissance spotted huge columns of German armour moving into position, indicating a large enemy counterattack was imminent. At that time, the British position across the Odon was precarious to say the least.

As skies cleared on 29 June the Allies re-commenced bombing raids and these greatly hindered the planned German counter-attack. The main assault didn't start until 18:00. Two hundred German panzers were thrown into the fight but the tight bocage limited the effectiveness of big tanks and by the end of the evening the attack fizzled out.

The British had blunted the cutting edge of German armour so badly there was no chance of them mounting any significant attacks on the Allied bridgehead. From this point of view the battle was a success, but Montgomery still did not have his hands on Caen.

Men of 12 Platoon, 'B' Company, 6th Royal Scots Fusiliers take cover in Saint-Manvieu-Norrey during Operation Epsom, Normandy, 26 June 1944.

'Our shelling is exploding just a hundred yards ahead of us, we are to advance a hundred yards every three minutes. Of course this brilliant plan failed as shells where falling short and we sustained our first casualties. Holding our weapons over our heads we walked to meet the enemy. They were everywhere popping up behind us and we were in one hell none of us could have possibly imagined. The fanatical young German SS men were certainly proving to be a force to reckon with. Nevertheless, due to tremendous barrage of gunfire pouring on them, we made progress to reach our target the village of St-Mauvieu'

Charles Hanaway, Bren Gunner,
6th Battalion, The Royal Scots Fusiliers

....

Tanks losses:
26 June – 1 July 1944

150

125

● **British forces**

● **German forces**

Casualties

c4,000

c3,000

90 The advance on Cherbourg

Cherbourg was one of the US Army's first major targets during Operation Overlord. The city at the end of the Cotentin Peninsula was a significant base for the occupying German forces. Capturing it would remove a threat from the Allies' rear before they advanced south. It would also give them access to major port facilities to unload supplies.

The defences of Cherbourg were designed to prevent an attack from the sea rather than from land. That said, the fortifications around the city were still formidable. The city was surrounded by a ring of concrete fortifications built on to three ridges that commanded every line of approach. In the city itself the arsenal was a powerful fortress, and the navy had built forts to defend the harbour.

Before attacking Cherbourg, the Allies launched a heavy aerial bombardment, pounding the city's defences. Then, at 14:00 on 22 June, the ground attack began.

The initial advance was tough for the Americans. Machine-guns stationed in concrete bunkers allowed the Germans to inflict heavy casualties while remaining safe from small arms fire. The Americans had to take out these strongpoints one at a time, but quickly came up with a strategy that was relatively effective. Using artillery and dive bombers to force the German defenders into their concrete pill-boxes and strongpoints,

the infantry would then pour fire into the strongholds while engineers would work their way to the rear, blowing open the doors and dropping in explosives or grenades. It was slow and dangerous work, but these tactics meant that the Americans were able to make steady progress. By early afternoon of 23 June, General Karl-Wilhelm von Schlieben – the man put in charge of keeping the Allies out of Cherbourg – reported into Field Marshal Rommel that the Americans had broken through the outer defences and were advancing towards the city. The next day he reported that he had committed his last reserves to the battle, including groups of non-combatants equipped with old French weapons. He also handed out a large number of Iron Crosses that had been dropped in by parachute, in an attempt to boost morale.

On 25 June, von Schlieben radioed Rommel to update him on the situation: 'Loss of the city shortly is unavoidable.... 2,000 wounded (are) without a possibility of being moved. Is the destruction of the remaining troops necessary as part of the general picture in view of the failure of effective counterattacks? Directive urgently requested.'

Later that afternoon the town was once more subjected to a naval bombardment. Von Schlieben radioed in again, 'I must state in the line of duty, that further sacrifices cannot alter anything.' To this, Rommel replied by radio, 'You will continue to fight until the last cartridge in accordance with the order from the Führer.'

General von Schlieben held out for as long as he could in the face of the Allied advance. He lived in a network of tunnels and bunkers filled with dust, smoke and the sound of generators. On 26 June, the powerful Fort du Roule fell and with it organised resistance in the city ceased. American tank destroyers started shooting into the tunnel entrances to von Schlieben's base. At last, he surrendered. General Omar Bradley, angry at the lives lost due to Schlieben's tenacity, and by his refusal to order a total surrender by the remaining Germans, refused to meet him.

Upon formal liberation, church bells rang out across the city and the jubilant population gave their liberators an enthusiastic welcome. On 27 June, thousands of Cherbourgeois acclaimed the victorious generals, grouped on the steps of the town hall.

Although Hitler had ordered von Rundstedt to consider a large armoured counterattack, Operation Epsom had drawn all available German reserves out to the east towards Caen. The Germans had no choice but to regroup and prepare for a war of attrition in an effort to confine the Allies to their beachhead.

US National Archives

Entrance to underground fortress in Cherbourg. It was here that Lieutenant General Carl Wilhelm von Schlieben, commander of the garrison at Cherbourg, and Rear Admiral Hennecke, gave themselves up a day before the general surrender.

Casualties

United States

2,800
killed

5,700
missing

13,500
wounded

Germany

c8,000
killed/missing

c30,000
captured

22,000

c38,000

Total

91 Operation Charnwood

As June turned into July, Caen still denied Montgomery. The city that was a strategic target for capture on D-Day itself was still in the hands of the 12th SS Panzer Division, commanded by Kurt 'Panzer' Meyer, backed up by the 16th Luftwaffe Field Division.

Previous Allied attempts to outflank and encircle Caen had failed, so Montgomery decided to change tactics and launch a full-frontal attack on the town in an attempt to overwhelm its defenders with sheer brute force. Montgomery therefore asked 115,000 men of his British 1st Corps, commanded by Lieutenant General Sir John Crocker, to take up the fight to Caen.

On the night of 7 July, 467 Lancaster and Halifax planes from RAF Bomber Command attacked Caen, dropping over 2,000 tonnes of bombs on the city. These planes were backed up by 656 artillery pieces and four warships (HMS *Roberts*, HMS *Belfast*, HMS *Emerald* and HMS *Rodney*) were also drafted in to give extra weight to the bombardment. At 04:30 on 8 July, under the protection of a creeping artillery barrage, the infantry advanced.

The relatively weak defences of the 16th Luftwaffe Field Division were brushed aside with minimal fuss but the 12th SS Panzer Division was an altogether tougher proposition. It required careful co-ordination of heavy artillery and big anti-tank guns to push the panzer back.

In the evening, Meyer gave the order for the 12th SS Panzers to retreat to the south of the city. The liberation of Caen was so very close.

The advance through the city continued the following day, with the German defenders using snipers and mortar units to good effect in an effort to slow down the Allies. By noon the 3rd British Infantry Division had reached the Orne's north bank, virtually destroying the remaining elements of the 16th Luftwaffe Field Division. A few hours later the British and Canadians met in the centre of the city and by 18:00 the northern half of Caen was firmly under Allied control. However, the huge bomb craters and rubble from the earlier bombardment had made it impossible for British armour to manoeuvre easily through the northern part of the city, preventing it from exploiting success.

Without possession of the terrain flanking the south of the city, no further gains could be made and the Operation was called to a halt. It had been an expensive two days with the attacking British 1st Corps losing approximately 3,800 men. The 12th SS Panzer Division was reduced to battalion strength and the 16th Luftwaffe Field Division was practically wiped out, losing three-quarters of its men.

Preliminary bombardment

In the preliminary bombardment, the Allies used

467 bombers,

656 artillery guns and

4 Royal Navy warships to smash Caen

Allied losses

The Anglo-Canadian forces that attacked Caen suffered

3,817 casualties and lost around

80 tanks and armoured vehicles

A young French woman distributes cherries to Canadian soldiers after the liberation of Caen.

George Rodger / Life Magazine

Three British soldiers in front of German propaganda posters.

George Rodger / Life Magazine

'The Tommy attacks with great masses of infantry and many tanks. We fight as long as possible but by the time the survivors try to pull back, we realise that we are surrounded'

Private Zimmer, 12th SS Panzer Division

92 The Battle for Saint-Lô

Immediately after the landings, after it was discovered that the Allies would not be able to immediately rampage through France, their main focus changed slightly to that of securing a safe beachhead to allow them to build up their numbers for the breakout into France. By the beginning of July this had been achieved and it was time to turn their attentions inland. The British Second Army looked to the town of Caen in the east as the gateway from which to break out of Normandy; the US First Army saw Saint-Lô as the door to central France.

The key to capturing Saint-Lô was the long Martinville Ridge, crowned by Hill 192, located about 5 miles northeast of the city. Named after its height in metres, Hill 192 was a strategically significant point in the battlefield. Perched on top, the Germans had an uninterrupted view north over the 2nd Division's lines, and to the west they overlooked the approaches that the 29th Division would need to use in their advance on the town. The big problem for the Americans was that the ridge and Hill 192 were covered in classic Normandy hedgerows. These tall narrow lanes were shrouded in thick vegetation that ranged anywhere from 4 feet to 9 feet in height and several feet deep, completely obstructing the view into the next field. Each tiny Norman field was enclosed by these ancient walls and became a veritable fortress for the defending Germans.

Following a savage fight on 11 July, during which the small hill was smashed by 45 tonnes of shells the 2nd Infantry Division finally secured this high ground, the 29th and 2nd Divisions were able to advance on the city without being overlooked.

That did not mean they would have an easy time of it. The German units defending Saint-Lô were the elite 3rd Parachute Division along with the remains of the 352nd Infantry Division who had caused such mayhem on Omaha Beach on D-Day. Experts in camouflage and trained to operate in small groups or alone, the German Paratroopers used the hedgerow terrain expertly to their advantage, forcing the Americans to pay dearly for every single metre of ground they captured.

On 16 July, after a bitter see-saw battle, the Americans took another strategic high point – Hill 122. From this vantage point they could see the whole of Saint-Lô below them.

The next day, the 3rd Battalion, 116th Infantry Regiment, commanded by Major Thomas D. Howie, began an advance before dawn to join up with the 2nd battalion at the hamlet of Martinville, one kilometre east of Saint-Lô. Despite machine-gun fire and the explosion of German mortar shells, Major Howie's men did not retaliate, so as to not give away their position. When the two battalions finally established a connection, shortly after dawn, Colonel Dwyer asked his men if they were able to continue to advance towards Saint-Lô. Major Howie replied by radio, confirming his men were able to advance. Moments later he was fatally wounded by German mortar fire.

On 18 July the 116th Infantry Regiment launched a final thrust into the town. By now the town had been virtually flattened and the majority of the 10,000 inhabitants had fled. The Americans formally entered Saint-Lô on 19 July, with the body of Major Howie placed on the hood of the lead jeep, symbolically making him the first American soldier to enter the city.

US National Archives

Two French boys watch Allied vehicles passing through the badly damaged city of Saint-Lô.

American Casualties for the period 7–22 July

29th Infantry Division:

3,706

30th Infantry Division:

3,934

35th Infantry Division:

2,437

Underground Hospital

In 1943, the Germans began digging an underground hospital, which remains today, using the slave labour of local French workers who were part of the Service du Travail Obligatoire

Awards for the town

On 2 June 1948, the municipality of Saint-Lô was awarded the French Légion d'Honneur and the Croix de Guerre 1939–1945 awards

93 Operation Goodwood

Operation Charnwood had taken Montgomery to the brink of capturing the elusive city of Caen, but the Germans were still clinging on to the south. Desperate to finish the job, General Montgomery met with General Omar Bradley and General Sir Miles Dempsey on 10 July about the next phase of the Allied breakout.

The plan was simple enough. Three armoured divisions – the Guards Armoured Division, the 7th Armoured Division and the 11th Armoured Division – would attack through a narrow corridor between the River Orne and the Bois de Bavent, fanning out as soon as there was space to do so. This attack would be supported by huge artillery support and over 2,000 heavy and medium bombers from both the Royal Air Force and the United States Army Air Force.

Detailed planning for Operation Goodwood started on 14 July, but the next day Montgomery issued a written directive ordering Dempsey to change the objectives of the operation from a 'deep break through' to a 'limited attack' in an effort to attract as much German armour as possible. battle for Normandy was spiralling into a bloody battle of attrition.

The first wave of bombers flew across enemy territory shortly before 06:00 on 18 July, shortly followed by an artillery bombardment. H-Hour was set for 07:45. Right on schedule the

artillery switched to a creeping barrage and the 11th Armoured Division started its advance.

Initial progress was good with the villages and towns of Hérouvillette-Escoville, Touffréville and Sannerville all liberated in relatively short order, but what had originally started out as a large assault by three armoured divisions had actually become an unsupported advance by just two tank regiments Meanwhile, the German defence systems had come to life and these two regiments were now finding themselves victims of heavy German fire. By mid-morning the advancing Divisions had joined back up with each other but it still took a day of tough fighting to finally capture Cagny.

While the British were advancing to the east of Caen, the Canadians were busy with their own operation to try and finally capture the southern areas of the city. After capturing a number of industrial suburbs to the south of Caen along the the Orne River, the Canadians turned their attention to the strategically important Verrières Ridge.

Though only 90 feet (27 metres) high, Verrières Ridge dominated the Caen–Falaise road and was stopping the Allies from breaking through to the south. The importance of the ridge was not lost on the German High Command and they had ordered the elite 1st SS Panzer Corps (commanded by Josef 'Sepp' Dietrich) to defend the area, along with elements of the 12th SS Panzer Division and the 1st SS Division Leibstandarte SS Adolf Hitler.

During the early hours of 20 July, the Canadians attacked the ridge. It was a disaster. Heavy rain prevented air support and made tank movement very difficult. Any progress was soon pinned down by German tank and artillery fire, and the South Saskatchewan Regiment was pushed back beyond its original starting-off point. The following day Canadian rein-forcements were sent on to the ridge to help stabilise the situation. Counterattack followed counterattack and although they had secured a number of footholds, they were by no means in control and had suffered over 1,300 casualties.

Operation Goodwood had been far from perfect, but it had indeed succeeded in attracting German armour to the east.

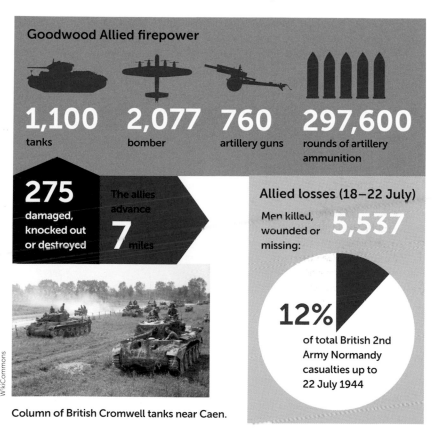

Goodwood Allied firepower

1,100 tanks

2,077 bomber

760 artillery guns

297,600 rounds of artillery ammunition

275 damaged, knocked out or destroyed

The allies advance **7** miles

Allied losses (18–22 July)

Men killed, wounded or missing: **5,537**

12% of total British 2nd Army Normandy casualties up to 22 July 1944

Column of British Cromwell tanks near Caen.

94 Operation Cobra

By early July there were real fears of a stalemate developing in Normandy. Churchill was becoming increasingly frustrated at the lack of progress and on 7 July Eisenhower wrote to Montgomery expressing his own concerns:

It appears to me that we must use all possible energy in a determined effort to prevent a stalemate or of facing the necessity of fighting a major defensive battle with the slight depth we how have in the bridgehead.

Subsequently, Montgomery asked both Bradley and Dempsey to come up with a plan to achieve the breakout – ideally concentrating forces onto a slightly narrower front to achieve the breakthrough.

Following this advice, Bradley devised a new plan for a major offensive. It was approved on 13 July and had a start date of 19 July. Operation Cobra was to utilise a heavy daylight air bombardment on a small piece of the front line 5 miles west of Saint-Lô, followed by an infantry attack moving south before turning west to cut off the defenders from the coast. Unfortunately, Sainte-Lô was not captured until 18 July and subsequent bad weather forced the Operation to be postponed. The attack finally went ahead properly during the morning of 25 July. More than 1,500 heavy bombers and 380 medium bombers smashed the German front line, but many of the bombs fell short, landing among the American forces and causing utter chaos – artillery observation posts were destroyed, telephone lines were cut and 601 men became casualties, 111 of which were fatal.

Eventually the Americans were able to reorganise themselves and launch their infantry attack. The positions of the opposing Panzer Lehr Division had been devastated, with over 1,000 men killed, tanks over turned and anti-tank positions smashed to pieces. As the American infantry began to move forward, the defenders could only offer feeble resistance. Indeed, the biggest obstacle was down to their own making – the bombing raids had smashed the ground up so badly that a large number of tanks fell into huge craters and were unable to get out again. Engineers quickly got to work in an effort to repair the roads; meanwhile the Germans began to recover began to put up some very stiff armoured resistance. By the end of the day the Americans had advanced just 2.5 miles (4 kilometres).

The next day General Collins decided to commit some more of his armour to the offensive with the US 2nd Armoured Division and the veteran 1st Infantry Division joining the attack. 26 July was a day of enemy roadblocks, armoured skirmishes and slow progress and by nightfall the Americans were still only half way to Coutances and the grand plan of Operation Cobra was beginning to fall apart.

US National Archives

US Troops and an M4 Sherman Tank Moving through the ruins of Coutances, 1944.

On the other side of the wire, the Germans were in bad shape. The Seventh Army had begun a general withdrawal and despite units of the 2nd and 17th SS Panzer Divisions attempting to construct a defensive line from Coutances via Cambernon to Savingy, German defences were collapsing. A desperate counterattack was launched but it was a failure. By the end of the day the Panzer Lehr Division was, according to German records, 'finally annihilated'. German troops abandoned their vehicles and fled on foot.

As the month closed, the German left flank had totally collapsed and the Americans were motoring down the coastline. By 30 July they had reached Avranches, some 27 miles (44 kilometres) south of Coutances. The taking of Avranches saw the end of bocage countryside. Now the US mechanised units could make full use of their speed and manoeuvrability, which had been so compromised by the terrain found in Normandy.

American Casualties

4,072
killed

23,779
wounded

German Casualties

2,500
killed

c20,000
prisoners

US National Archives

Greyhounds of Company 'C' 82nd Recon Battalion, 2nd Armored Division pass through the road junction at Saint-Sever Calvados.

As they crowded into holding areas across the south of England, awaiting the call to begin embarkation, many men, aware that they may not make it through the coming hours or days, began to write notes and letters to wives, mothers and sweethearts. Lieutenant Ian Hammerton, a British officer commanding a Flail Tank Troop, noticed that his men wrote 'letters of farewell we hoped would never have to be sent'.

The majority of the letters were simple notes that contained basic facts and details, as the men knew that every word they wrote would be inspected by the censors.

Aboard the USS *Chase*, photographer Robert Capa observed that the men with whom he was sharing the journey to Normandy could be split into three distinct groups: the gamblers, the planners and the writers. The gamblers were on the upper deck, huddled around small blankets, watching as hundreds of dollars exchanged hands on the roll of a couple of dice.

The planners were below deck, studying maps of the beaches and the terrain of the ground beyond the landing zone on which they would land. They would stare at models for hours, memorising the topography and making notes of safe areas.

The last group were the writers who 'hid in corners and put down beautiful sentences on paper leaving their favourite shotguns to kid brothers and their dough to the family'.

Once the landings had taken place and the invasion was in full swing, Allied soldiers and sailors were so busy that they barely had time to scribble down a few hasty sentences to reassure loved ones back home that they were alright. Lieutenant John Pelly was serving as a midshipman onboard the British destroyer HMS *Eglington:*

```
June 7

Not a minute to spare except you can probably guess how life is with
us these days - damn busy and tired, but very well. Don't worry.
```

Writing home was not just confined to Allied soldiers, of course. Millions of Wehrmacht soldiers also put pen (or pencil) to paper regularly to keep their family and loved-ones up to date on their well-being.

Josef B: Wehrmacht Staff Sergeant in Normandy, wrote:

June 6

Now finally the hour has come. How did you react to the news about the invasion? Although it had to happen and was foreseeable, it impressed me a lot. Of course, it is not a trifle. For sure these hours the hugest battle is taking place that the world has ever seen. Hopefully fortune is with us now. Now history is being made. All the words are really just air. It's all about acting. Especially now I feel so unimportant and small. The days to come are certainly going to put an end to the suspense.

V-Mail letter sent by Private Harry Schiraldi, a medic from New York who served with the 116th Infantry Regiment, 29th Infantry Division. On the morning of the invasion, Schiraldi was killed by machine-gun fire on Omaha Beach

To reduce the cost of transferring an original paper letter through the military postal system, a V-mail (known as Victory Mail) letter would be censored, copied to microfilm for the journey back to America and printed back to paper upon arrival at its destination. This process saved much needed space onboard US cargo ships. V-Mail was free to all American soldiers serving overseas

96 Normandy American Cemetery & Memorial, Colleville-sur-Mer

The Normandy American Cemetery and Memorial in France is located on top of the bluffs that overlook Omaha Beach, just outside Colleville-sur-Mer. The site is maintained by the American Battle Monuments Commission (ABMC) on the site of the temporary American St Laurent Cemetery, established by the US First Army on 8 June 1944 as the first American cemetery on European soil in World War 2.

The site was designed by Harbeson, Hough, Livingston & Larson – an architectural firm based out of Philadelphia – and covers 172.5 acres. Contained within the cemetery are the graves of 9,380 American servicemen and women, most of whom lost their lives in the D-Day landings and ensuing operations.

The names of 1,557 Americans who lost their lives in the Normandy campaign but could not be located and/or identified are inscribed on the walls of a semi-circular garden towards the east of the memorial. Here there is also a 22-foot-high bronze statue entitled *The Spirit of American Youth Rising from the Waves* by Donald De Lue, and an overhead mural by Leon Kroll. An orientation table overlooking the beach depicts the landings in Normandy.

In 2007, the Normandy Visitors' Centre opened. Costing $30 million, it was officially opened on 6 June during the commemoration of the 63rd Anniversary of D-Day. The centre is sited in a wooded area of the cemetery approximately 100 meters to the east of the Garden of the Missing.

Dug into the lawn opposite the entrance of the old visitors' building is a sealed time capsule, which contains news reports from 6 June 1944. The capsule is covered by a pink granite slab upon which is engraved: 'To be opened 6 June 2044'. Drilled into the centre of this slab is a bronze plaque carrying the following inscription:

In memory of General Dwight D. Eisenhower and the forces under his command. This sealed capsule containing news reports of the June 6, 1944 Normandy landings is placed here by the newsmen who were here, June 6, 1969.

The Normandy American Cemetery is the ABMC's most visited cemetery, receiving approximately one million visitors each year.

The Normandy American Cemetery is the final resting place for more than 9,000 Americans who gave their lives in World War 2.

The cemetery covers

172.5 acres

1,557

names are inscribed on the 'Walls of the Missing'

9,380

US military graves – most of whom were killed during the D-Day landings and ensuing operations

Embedded in the lawn is a time capsule containing news reports from 6 June 1944

† = 10 graves

97 *Deutscher Soldatenfriedhof, La Cambe*

The size of the US war cemetery at Colleville-sur-Mer is vast, but it is not the largest cemetery in the area. That dubious honour goes to the Deutscher Soldaten-friedhof (German Military Cemetery) at La Cambe. This vast graveyard is the final resting place for over 21,000 German soldiers, killed either during the Allied invasion or in the subsequent fighting in the Normandy area.

The site was originally established by the United States Army Graves Registration Service during the war and became the resting place for both American and German fallen, buried in two adjacent fields. After the conclusion of war in 1945, the Americans transferred two-thirds of their dead back to the US in accordance with the wishes of their families, whilst the remainder were moved to the permanent American Cemetery at Colleville-sur-Mer. Meanwhile, the German dead, who were scattered all over Normandy, were slowly consolidated into the La Cambe site. In 1948, La Cambe had around 8,000 German graves but in the following decade the remains of a further 12,000 German soldiers where moved here from 1,400 different locations across Normandy.

La Cambe was officially inaugurated as a German War Cemetery in September 1961. Since that date, the remains of more than 700 soldiers have been found on battlefields across Normandy and reinterred at La Cambe.

Today there are 21,222 burials at La Cambe, with 207 belonging to unknown soldiers. Two notable burials at La Cambe are SS-Sturmbannführer Adolf Diekmann, the most senior officer at the massacre in Oradour-sur-Glane, who was killed in action on 29 June 1944, and SS-Hauptsturmführer Michael Wittmann, the tank commander who, along with his crew, was killed on 8 August 1944. The remains of Wittmann and his crew were discovered in 1983 and reinterred together at La Cambe.

Calvados Tourism

A grave at *Deutscher Soldatenfriedhof*.

A visitor centre was established in the mid-1990s, providing information on the German losses during Operation Overlord. Visitors can also view a permanent exhibition about the German War Graves Commission and access a database to locate the graves of dead German military personnel. A peace garden with 1,200 maple-trees is adjacent to the cemetery and offers quiet walks for thoughtful reflection.

VOLKSBUND

Gemeinsam für den Frieden.

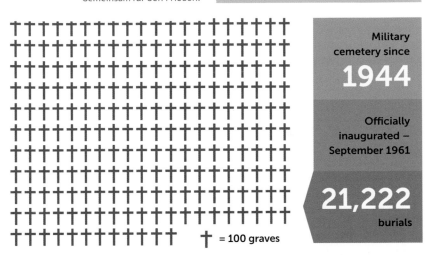

The majority of the German war dead buried at La Cambe fell between 6 June and 20 August 1944, and their ages range from 16 to 72

Military cemetery since
1944

Officially inaugurated – September 1961

21,222
burials

✝ = 100 graves

207
of the men are unknown and are buried together in a mass grave

Notable burials

Generalmajor Sigismund-Helmut von Dawans, killed in the RAF raid on the Panzergruppe West's GHQ

SS-Sturmbannführer Adolf Diekmann, the most senior officer at the massacre of Oradour-sur-Glane on 10 June 1944. Ordered to be court-martialled, he was killed in battle in Normandy on 29 June

Unlike the American and Commonwealth War Graves Commissions, the German Commission is entirely voluntary and relies on gifts and collections to further its work. During the summer months one may see international school children tending the graves. They volunteer to work with the Volksbund during their school holidays and visit American and German war cemeteries, memorials and sites of the invasion, and take part in the memorial ceremony with veterans and the Mayor of La Cambe.

98 Juno Beach Centre

June 1994 was the 50th anniversary of D-Day and a trip was organised for the men of the 14th Field Regiment (Royal Canadian Artillery) to retrace the route travelled through France, Belgium and Holland by their regiment half a century earlier. After taking part in this trip, veterans of the regiment suggested that a trip to Normandy be planned the following year for their children and grandchildren. They wondered what they would be able to show their families aside from the beach with tourists, streets named after Canadians and the markers, monuments and cemeteries.

And so was sown the idea of building a Canadian museum in Normandy. A large fundraising campaign was undertaken in Canada to secure funds which won the backing of the Canadian government and some of the country's largest corporations. After many years of fundraising, construction finally began on 1.5 hectares of land made available by the town of Courseulles-sur-Mer, and on 6 June 2003 the Juno Beach Centre was officially opened by D-Day Veteran Garth Webb, one of the key figures behind the concept, design and fundraising programmes that enabled the Centre to become reality.

Shortly after the creation of the Juno Beach Centre, the Juno Beach Centre Association (JBCA) wanted a way to reach out to Canadian educators and give them added motivation to continue teaching the history of World War 2 and Remembrance in their classes. The idea of a ten-day tour of the battlefields in France was a natural extension of the educational and memorial mission of the Juno Beach Centre. In 2005, the first of these annual tours took place. It has run every year since and over 300 educators from across Canada have taken part.

Today, the Juno Beach Centre is what the veterans wanted it to be: a place of education providing a better understanding of the contribution Canada made during World War 2, not just the Normandy landings. At the same time, by showcasing today's Canada, it is a place where visitors from all around the world learn more about Canadian values and culture. In this respect, the Centre stands as both the Canadian World War 2 memorial and education centre in Europe and as a testament to the veterans who helped build it. The Minister of Canadian Heritage has designated Juno Beach as a site of national historic significance to Canada.

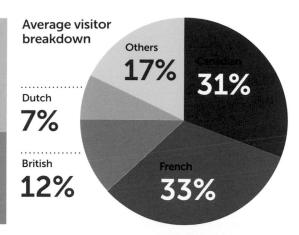

Average visitor breakdown

Others 17%

Canadian 31%

Dutch 7%

British 12%

French 33%

Over **1,000** Canadian veterans attended the opening ceremony in 2003

50,000 visitors a year on average

Calvados Tourisme

Calvados Tourisme

Alamy

99 La Voie de la Liberté (Liberty Road)

The Liberty Road (La Voie de la Liberté) follows the route of the Allied forces from their initial breakout from the beachheads on 6 June 1944 towards Sainte-Marie-du-Mont, across Northern France to Metz and then north up to the Belgian town of Bastogne. The route covers 1,146 kilometres, and after each and every kilometre there is a decorative stone marker or 'Borne'. The first one (numbered 00) is situated just beside the landing zone area at Utah Beach.

Soon after the end of World War 2, Guy de la Vasselais, French liaison officer to US General George S. Patton, suggested the idea of installing distinctive markers placed at intervals along the roads followed by Patton's US Third Army during its advance through Western Europe.

La Voie de la Liberté was officially opened on 17 September 1947 in the presence of many French, American and Allied dignitaries at Fontainebleau, although the process of designing and implementing these Bornes was not without incident. The mayor of Sainte-Marie-du-Mont petitioned to have the very first Borne (number '0') built at the disembarkation site on Utah Beach but the French Government had already decided that marker zero should be positioned outside the town hall in Sainte-Mère-Église. Not to be outdone, the mayor had his own marker made which was 10 per cent bigger than the official Bornes and gave it the number '00'. Despite the tussle regarding where the Liberty Road should begin, it stretches out through France following the advance of General Patton, travelling through the cities of Sainte-Marie-du-Mont, Saint-Malo, Rennes, Angers, Le Mans, Chartres, Fontainebleau, Reims, Verdun and Metz, then on through Luxembourg before finishing at Bastogne. The design of the marker was carried out by sculptor François Cogné and carries several symbolic elements, including the Flaming Torch of Liberty, emerging from the sea and being carried towards the east. Along the circumference of each milestone's dome-shaped top are forty-eight stars representing the (then) forty-eight states of America, and there is also a nod to the US Third Army.

0 or 00

Originally the government stipulated that Borne 0 (the start of the Liberty Road) would be situated outside the Sainte-Mère-Église town hall. However, the Mayor of Sainte-Marie-du-Mont wanted the route to start at Utah Beach and commissioned his own, bigger Borne and gave it the number 00. This Borne marks the spot where General Theodore Roosevelt Jr landed on D-Day

WikiCommons

Borne number 00, on the sands of Utah Beach.

Borne design

The sculptor François Cogné designed the milestones, which are placed at an interval of 1 km along the Liberty Road.

Each milestone is

1.20m

tall and weighs

435kg

A crown of

48

stars symbolising the 48 states of America (Alaska and Hawaii joined in 1959) marks their top

The four red sections placed beneath the stars represent the four sections of the Road to Freedom:

1. Sainte-Mère-Église–Cherbourg
2. Sainte-Mère-Église–Avranches
3. Avranches–Metz
4. Metz–Luxembourg–Bastogne

The name and inauguration date of the road is printed in blue, just above the Torch of Liberty

The torch is embossed with the emblem of General Patton's Third US Army

The Borne's base is blue and symbolises the waves of the Atlantic Ocean

UNESCO

...ing to a statement issued by ...e's Culture Ministry in January 2018, ...roposal has been accepted for the ...ntire D-Day invasion coastline (some 30 miles of coast between Ravenoville and Ouistreham) to be declared a World Heritage Site.

French officials have been actively seeking World Heritage status for the beaches since 2006.

The Culture Ministry stated: 'This site, proposed for inscription on UNESCO's World Heritage List, preserves the traces and bears the memory of a combat for liberty and peace.'

The official recommendation submitted by the French authorities includes not just the beaches, but all elements of the Atlantic Wall; including the battery at Longues-sur-Mer, the Pointe du Hoc, the remains of the artificial Mulberry Harbour, all related shipwrecks off the Normandy coast and any associated memorials and cemeteries in the immediate area.

The proposal is expected to be discussed at the World Heritage Committee's meeting in the 75th anniversary year of the landings. If the invasion coastline is successful and makes it on to the list of World Heritage Sites, it would ensure the long-term conservation, improve global awareness and allow new educational initiatives to be developed.

It would truly be a fitting final 'moment' for the D-Day invasion area.

The Crisbecq Battery, nr Utah Beach with 210 mm Skoda gun.

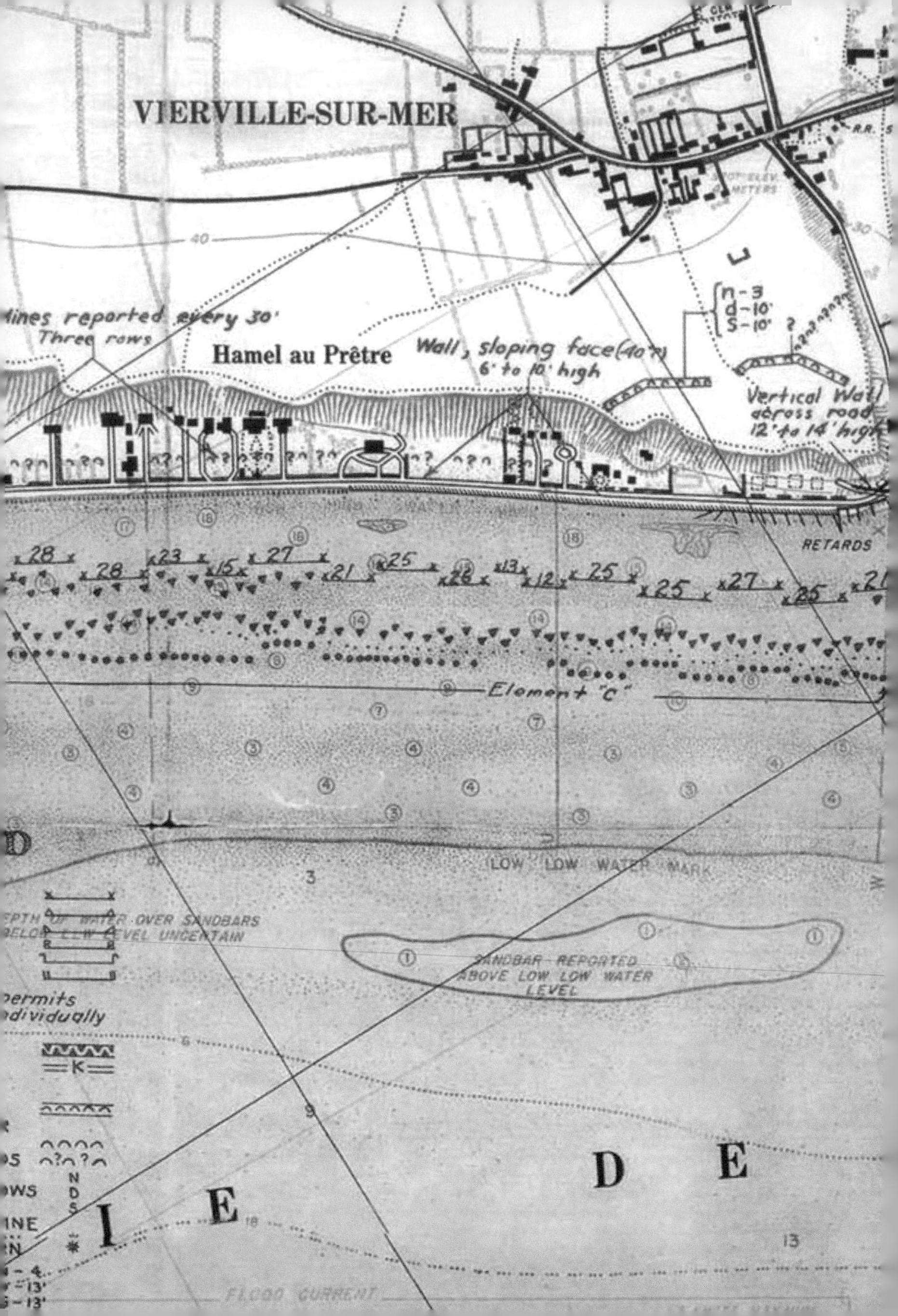

VIERVILLE-SUR-MER

Mines reported every 30'
Three rows

Hamel au Prêtre

Wall, sloping face (40°)
6' to 10' high

n - 3
d - 10'
S - 10' ?

Vertical Wall
across road
12' to 14' high

RETARDS

28   28   23   15   27   21   25   26   13   12   25   25   27   25   21

Element "C"

LOW LOW WATER MARK

3

DEPTH OF WATER OVER SANDBARS
BELOW LLW LEVEL UNCERTAIN

permits
individually

K

SANDBAR REPORTED
ABOVE LOW LOW WATER
LEVEL

D E

I E

FLOOD CURRENT

13